Man Without Tears

Soundings for a Christian Anthropology

Christopher F. Mooney, S.J.

Man Without Tears
Soundings for a Christian Anthropology

HARPER & ROW, PUBLISHERS
New York   Evanston
San Francisco
London

Chapter One has appeared with some slight differences in *Teilhard de Chardin: In Quest of the Perfection of Man,* ed. Geraldine O. Browning, Fairleigh Dickinson University Press, 1973.

References to the Bible, unless otherwise indicated, are excerpts from the NEW AMERICAN BIBLE, copyright © 1970 Confraternity of Christian Doctrine used by permission of copyright owner.

ACKNOWLEDGMENTS

Grateful acknowledgment is made to the following for permission to reprint copyrighted material:

A.P. WATT & SON for excerpts from the *Psalms: A New Translation,* copyright © by A.P. Watt & Son. Used with permission of The Grail (England) and William Collins, Sons & Co., Ltd.

DELACORTE PRESS/SEYMOUR LAWRENCE for excerpts from *Cat's Cradle* by Kurt Vonnegut, Jr., copyright © 1963 by Kurt Vonnegut, Jr., by arrangement with Delacorte Press/Seymour Lawrence.

LEEDS MUSIC CORPORATION for excerpts from "Jesus Christ Superstar" by Weber & Rice.

OXFORD UNIVERSITY PRESS for "Spring and Fall" by Gerard Manley Hopkins, copyright © 1967, from the 4th Edition, edited by W. H. Gardner and M. H. MacKenzie.

SHEED & WARD for excerpts from *The Holy Bible* translated by Ronald Knox, copyright 1946 by permission of Sheed & Ward, New York.

Library of Congress Cataloging in Publication Data

Mooney, Christopher F   1925–
    Man without tears. 148p. ; 21cm.
    Bibliography: p. 137-148.
    1. Man (Theology) I. Title.
BT701.2.M57   233   74–25705
ISBN 0-06-065921-1

75 76 77 78 79 10 9 8 7 6 5 4 3 2 1

To Aunt Nell
in her ninety-sixth year

Contents

	Introduction	I
1	Survival	II
2	Conflict	28
3	Play	46
4	Failure	64
5	Old Age	82
6	Death	100
7	Christ	118
	Notes	137

Introduction

The pages which follow were written in the belief that the most important function of theology today is to illumine the element of mystery in human life. The aim is therefore the very opposite of that of the modern technocrat, who believes that human fear and self-doubt are rooted outside the person, and that the only thing needed to dispel anxiety is a technological solution to problems of hunger, population, ecology, and war.

Such control is actually achieved in the fictional future of Pierre Boulle's *Desperate Games*,[1] but his sharp satire envisions a strange resulting malady. The disease is eventually diagnosed as loss of confidence in the ego. It renders a highly trained astronaut incapable of landing his private plane in perfect weather; a vacationing accountant, separated from his calculators, incapable of counting his money and paying his bill. The victims, long accustomed to having machines think for them, transfer their normal self-confidence to confidence in the infallible mechanical devices provided by science. With machines more important than people, an all-pervasive melancholy begins to appear. Millions come to see life as meaningless, and the suicide rate takes an alarming leap. In the end desperate measures are resorted to by the ruling scientists to remedy what they see as a failure of control. Boulle's point is that the other side of the newly discovered autonomy of the human creature is the inevitable increase, in direct proportion to its freedom, of that sense of contingency and finiteness which are the ultimate sources of despair. This Job-experience, as Kierkegaard calls it, may no longer force people to turn to God as it so often did in the past, but it can still make them painfully aware that there is much in life they do not yet fully understand.

"No man is wiser than Socrates," said the oracle at Delphi, which Socrates interpreted as meaning: "He is wisest who like Socrates knows that his wisdom is in truth worth nothing." And later in the *Apology* Socrates contends that the unexamined life is not worth living. But what would he say today to men and women who fear that they do not possess, and may never possess, the wisdom to examine their own lives well? The new concept of freedom born at the end of the eighteenth century released the human race from bondage to any patterns discernible either in nature or in the cosmos. But the problem then became how the human could serve as a standard for individual life. The religious side of this question has been the phenomenon of secularization, that historical process whereby human experience became detached from any religious base: religion was no longer needed to support values and institutions which could no longer support themselves. Whatever meanings there were in life suddenly had to stand on their own. The ambiguities of love, the anguish of sickness and disease, the struggle between good and evil in the heart, the psychological crises of youth, middle years, old age, and death, all these became questions to which there were no longer facile answers. Secularity as a spirit and life-style inevitably also affected the self-understanding of the churches themselves: serious Christians gradually came to share in the doubts of the world. They recognized at last that it is not at all easy to say what "God" means; or to discern when orthodox formulas of Christology have become empty and when not, or how reform of church structures can avoid being seen as mostly irrelevant. Believers thus began to think of themselves as in part also unbelievers. Face to face with the secular, they too had to be guarded from the twofold temptation of idolatry and despair.

Men and women today, therefore, whether religiously oriented or not, have to strive much harder than their precursors to form some pattern out of the disparate experiences of life. Faced with a welter of conflicting meanings and ideologies, which they can neither assimilate nor evaluate, they may well settle for that "Protean" outlook described by Robert J. Lifton. "Protean man" eschews any set of choices which would force him to adopt one single stance among many. As a psychological type he is addicted to change rather than stability—after the Greek god Proteus who easily changed shape and appearance but vigorously resisted committing himself to any single form, especially that of his true self. Because consistency of self-image is neither imposed nor enforced by society today, the temptation is strong to legitimize the experiences of internal tension and cognitive overload by appealing to the madness and confusion of the world outside. What then results is a kind of "psychohistorical dislocation" from the vital symbols of tradition, including religious symbols, from which one no longer draws nourishment. Rapid alterations in life-style and beliefs thus become an attempt to keep pace with this crumbling of symbolic boundaries which previously constituted one's personal and religious identity. The individual's sense of "territoriality" gets violated, and this in turn gives rise to a continual quest for new boundaries. Such a situation, says Lifton, because it tends to erode at a very deep level the sense of self as a continuing moral entity, is the reason one often encounters in Protean man a strong ideological hunger, since he is starved for ideas and feelings that can give coherence to his world. Like Richard R. Niebuhr's "radial man," his desire to travel light is one of his hallmarks: he does not want his journeying encumbered by images and formulations of belief which do not touch his deepest center. But his hunger is always unsatisfied because he is not at all sure where or what that deepest center is.[2]

One extreme of the Protean life-style is exemplified by the type of person Philip Rieff calls "therapeutic" man. According to Rieff, the therapeutic not only avoids moral demands made upon him by others, but tries to do away as much as possible with what he feels to be "the tyranny of moral passion as the inner dynamic of social order." If this is the man of the future, says Rieff, then his triumph will tend to do away with the present waste of energy taking place through love, hatred, hope, and despair. "That a sense of well-being has become the end, rather than the by-product of striving after some superior communal end, announces a fundamental change of focus in the entire cast of our culture."³ "Well-being" here means knowing how to live with self-control and psychic balance, how prudently to seek enjoyment in an affluent society, and how to be skeptical about almost everything. Stable identity in any political, religious, or economic sense is a nonvalue. Rigorous commitments are not necessarily ruled out, as long as these are short-term and are seen as pleasurable and meaningful enough to warrant some limited investment of energy. But blind loyalty in any form is inconsistent with the quest for variety and richness of experience. While religious man was born to be saved, says Rieff, therapeutic man was born to be pleased. If he is unheroic, without enthusiasm for causes of any kind, he is also free from cruelty and self-deception. His particular form of Protean life is the clearest instance that modern self-understanding is becoming more personal, individualized, and privatized. It also exemplifies the great risk of such a psychological approach, namely the total loss of any sense of life's mystery, any sense that certain events are utterly beyond our ability either to understand or control, any sense that humankind is capable of reaching heights of grandeur and ecstacy as well as misery and despair.

How is one to speak of such mystery to Protean man? How is one to help him find the deepest center of himself? Certainly not through the highly intellectualized language of traditional theology. "Nothing influences our conduct less than do intellectual ideas," writes Jung. An idea molds man, he adds, only when it is the expression of psychic experience and represents forces that are beyond logical justification.[4] If Christian realities are to have any meaning today they must therefore be approached from and through the impact they have upon human existence. Such a perspective does not mean making the human being the measure of all things. It means simply that we can have no religious knowledge which is not somehow grounded in experience. We can only speak of "revelation" when our consciousness can actually take in what is revealed and express it in language and life. For years now Karl Rahner has advocated an "anthropological theology."[5] What this approach avoids is any idea that God must continuously interfere in history from outside it, like a clumsy artisan who feels he has to improve upon his first sketchy plans. God's activity, in other words, does not compete with ours. He does not reach us from without inward, said the Flemish mystic Ruysbroeck, but from within outward, from the very center and core of our existence. He is "intimior intimo meo," to use Augustine's phrase, "more inward to me than the most inward part of me."[6] Or to use a formula of Teilhard de Chardin: "Properly speaking, God does not make things; he makes things make themselves."[7]

The human thus has God in its definition. If it sometimes baffles and overwhelms us, this is because it is meant to image a mysterious and ineffable God. From a Christian point of view there is no such thing as an autonomous man or woman with God as object. The Protean lives of today are therefore no less under God's influence than the more stable and committed lives of the past. Whatever relationships men and women may have with God must come from and through their experiences here and now. If our age is dominated by adherence to the immediate and the concrete, then it is there that God is to be found. If the human has become autonomous, then this autonomy has to be in some way due to God, a creation of the secular by the sacred, as it were. Hence it makes no sense at all to see the present situation as a quarrel between religious man on the one hand and secular man on the other. Whatever is happening is going on within one and the same person. Religious people cannot escape the fact that all their energies are framed within the secular project, and neither can those who are thoroughly secular escape the presence of God at work in the depths of their being.[8]

The task faced by a Christian anthropology, then, is to search out meaning for those events of life in which, because of our total involvement, the creative action of God is known through faith to be operative. This is no easy thing, for to ask questions about ultimate meaning is to recognize that the element of surprise cannot be eliminated from life, that there can be no insurance policy against what is often called chance but which Christians call providence. Eventually this type of inquiry leads to a sense of threat, helplessness, and limitation well described by Pascal: "When I consider the brief span of my life, absorbed in the eternity of time which went before and will come after it, the tiny space that I occupy and even that I see, plunged in the infinite immensity of the spaces which I do not know and which do not know me, I am terrified and astonished to find myself here rather than there, for there is no reason why I should be here rather than there, why now rather than then. Who put me here? By whose order and design were this place and time allotted to me?"[9] How is one to support such awareness of fragility and insignificance? Are we of no importance at all? Is there nothing in life over which to exercise our passion for control?

Next to the power of love, writes Langdon Gilkey, meaning is the most precious gift destiny can bestow upon us. The ability to experience and actualize it is what enables us to continue living with serenity and courage and is thus one of the chief manifestations of grace in natural life. "A sense of the significance of what we do comes unearned, quietly, and without our bidding, for we cannot establish it. It is the condition and not the result of our willing and our action. . . . The love of something as worthful cannot be willed, but is the basis of all willing. It is therefore one of those givens in life on which our creativity and values are founded."[10] The proper act of those who have received without doing is therefore thanksgiving. This is why a change in oneself, a gradual new birth, a sense of meaning for the future, are the chief reasons people have been led to speak of the providence of God. Einstein once remarked that God is subtle but not malicious. Nowhere is this subtlety more manifested than in the contrast between those who are able and those who are unable to accept with happiness and gratitude the mysterious and fragile meaning of what is.

But one must have some idea what these meanings are. This book is an attempt to explore some of them as they appear in certain contemporary experiences. Each chapter is intended as a "sounding," an effort to measure the depth of a given experience using the weight of Christian revelation. If one asks why these seven experiences were chosen rather than seven others, the answer must be personal: over the last few years I have in some way been involved in all the experiences I have attempted to describe. As one may gather from the preceding paragraphs, I conceive the fundamental religious problem today to be the fact that modern culture has become more and more secularized while religious men and women seeking to relate to it have traditionally not been secular in their outlook at all. This has inevitably caused all sorts of identity crises, and has served to bring out the Protean creature which inhabits each one of us. In the past one's religious identity was presumed to rest upon more or less unchanging conceptual formulas and practices as well as tight juridical structures. Becoming seriously involved in secular culture, however, means challenging such formulas and practices and breaking away from such structures, since their origin was a culture very different from our own. Formulas, practices, and customs are surely necessary for any religion to mediate the vision of its founder, but these are necessarily conditioned by the times that give them birth, and so will inevitably incorporate whatever presuppositions are then current regarding the relationship of sacred to profane. New understanding of this relationship must therefore give rise to new formulas and structures.

One's religious identity is thus a lived reality of which one can never be in full possession, an outgrowth of continuity and discontinuity with one's past. I personally feel it to be more important to risk a false identity than not to be open to a new one. For life is never simple and sure, but rather messy and uncertain, as it was for Jesus himself—full of problems as well as opportunities. Unfortunately many a committed Christian is unaware that the challenge is to exploit the opportunities and not merely to solve the problems. On the other hand, if we actually do accept this challenge, we then have to ask ourselves how genuine commitment to a culture is possible without at the same time becoming identified with it—without losing our ability as Christians to be critical of its values. Hence the need we have of not losing contact with our religious tradition. For such contact forces that Protean part of us to scrutinize our value system and to acknowledge the fact that there are no technical answers to moral problems. However, while our prayer thus becomes an exercise of our critical function, it will inevitably bring along with it, sooner or later, acute embarrassment at our inadequacy and the acknowledgment that we do not really care for God, that our religious need is utterly feeble. This is why Abraham Heschel could say that true religion is an answer to the question: Who needs man? At root it is an awareness of being needed, of man being a need of God. This kind of awareness is not easy to come by, and reaching it may be a long journey for "Protean man." In the end, however, such a person is not likely to be puzzled about who or what he really is.

The seven chapters that follow all flesh out one or other of these themes, finding them first in experiences which are social and then in those more concerned with the individual. For the opening discussion I have focused upon contemporary concern for the future through the eyes of one who has substantially altered my own sense of identity as a Christian, Pierre Teilhard de Chardin. More vigorously than any other writer in his lifetime he opted for the primacy of human self-consciousness, thereby establishing man as the axis of the evolutionary process, while never losing sight of his biological link to the world of matter. The fact that the human race is still in its adolescence and the discoveries of science still in their infancy meant for him that the mystery of life and matter is far greater than we ever suspected, and that our fears for the future will be in direct proportion to our capacity for knowledge and control. Chapter 2 pursues another aspect of this openness to development: our ability to dream of different futures and to actualize these dreams of the new in spite of the pull of inertia toward things as they are. I became concerned for this role of utopia in human life through the growing movements of protest against various forms of oppression. The reader should know, however, that while I speak here about the oppressed, I am not so presumptuous as to speak for them; I am too much part of the bourgeois society under attack for fostering oppression, and am also well aware that the oppressed can and do speak very well for themselves. My aim has been simply to situate the world's conflict and struggle within the larger eschatological search for the new humanity. For I believe that the task of theology here is not to legitimize some ideology of social change but to expose the religious roots of the human thirst for justice, thereby providing the occasion within Christian churches themselves for the promotion and renewal of freedom.

From a more individual point of view, I turn in Chapter 3 to our relief from struggle through play and festivity, which until recently have rarely had their religious significance tested. I write about them as one who relishes their anticipation rather than their spontaneity, but who nonetheless puts high value upon the surprising and unexpected. Chapter 4 began through my involvement in the demise of Woodstock College, the oldest and best of the Jesuit theological schools in America. Its closing, due to policy decisions within the Jesuit Order over which its faculty and students had no control, forced me to ask about those many times in life when each of us is judged and found wanting. "Life is essentially a cheat," said F. Scott Fitzgerald, "and its conditions are those of defeat." I wanted to inquire to what extent the second statement could be true without warranting the harsh conviction of the first.

This led me naturally to deal in the following chapter with what Charles de Gaulle once called "the shipwreck of old age." I often visit an elderly aunt, to whom this book is dedicated and who has grown into her mid-nineties with keen faculties, relatively good health, and a charming sense of humor. She inspires others both as a person and as a Christian—a woman of deep faith in God and confidence in the power of prayer. Yet she could say to me one day, after we visited some other old people, "This old age, it's a terrible thing that God does to us, isn't it?" In a sense the whole chapter is about her, though I never mention her name. Finally there are the questions of death and the humanity of Christ in Chapters 6 and 7, both exemplifying the most extraordinary extremes of contingency and transcendence. They also involve factual data of the most compelling kind, not at all congenial to the theologizing of a former age. Both try to come to grips with our frantic human search for significance and hope; they envision a day when this search will finally end. "On that day," said Jesus, "you will have no questions to ask me."[11]

Two colleagues and friends, Bartholomew J. Collopy, S.J., and Leo J. O'Donovan, S.J., helped greatly with their encouragement and sharp criticism of each chapter, and I want to express my special gratitude to them. I am grateful also to Helen Zeccola for proofreading the entire manuscript and to Katherine Kendall for typing and retyping the text with both patience and accuracy. Finally I want to thank my cousin, Richard Mooney, for his sound advice on a particularly difficult section of the book.

I

Survival

Some extraordinary judgments have recently been made on the significance of what is currently taking place in human consciousness. "We are experiencing one of the great revolutionary transformations of mankind," writes Princeton historian C. E. Black. "The process of change in the modern era is of the same order of magnitude as that from prehuman to human life and from primitive to civilized societies."[1] Sir George Thompson, Nobel Prize physicist and author of *The Foreseeable Future,* believes that man's cultural development is now so rapid that to understand it we have to think in terms of an event such as the invention of agriculture in the neolithic age. One clear symptom of what is going on is that mass neurosis which Alvin Toffler has christened "future shock": an acute sense of stress and disorientation induced by the experience of too much change in too short a time. The human race is being asked to adapt psychically to phenomena it does not yet understand, and its ability to do so is being taxed beyond healthy limits. Above all we experienced the fear that we are not going to adapt at all: the premature arrival of the future frightens us precisely because it is premature and we ourselves unprepared. Accustomed for centuries to measure change in terms of institutional development and economic growth, we are now being forced for the first time to evaluate our history in terms of what is going on inside us. For it is our consciousness, that most inclusive of interior realities, that is undergoing major displacement, and we are not at all sure whether this change is for the better or for the worse.

At least one serious thinker, Pierre Teilhard de Chardin, believed that it is for the better. "We now have to accept it as proven," he wrote as early as 1936, "that mankind has just entered into what is probably the most extensive period of transformation it has known since its birth. . . . Today something is happening to the whole structure of human consciousness: a fresh kind of life is beginning to appear."[2] Far from being the result of a naïve optimism, this conviction of Teilhard arose from a very keen sense of the harsh realities of life and the risks of human freedom. The forces of counterculture moving toward fragmentation and dispersal were vivid realities for him. On the occasion of a friend's death he once exclaimed: "What an absurd thing life is, looked at superficially! It is so absurd that you feel yourself thrown back upon a stubborn, desperate faith in the reality of spirit and its survival. Otherwise (if there were no such thing as spirit, I mean) we should have to be idiots not to call off the whole human effort."[3] His explanation of our present experience is consequently a highly complex and nuanced one, intimately linked to the Christian message of universal love and the community of all human beings with the person of Jesus.

Teilhard said quite explicitly that the ultimate grounds for man's hope in the future must be religious, since such grounds alone can provide the strong ethical drive to *act* in the present crisis, as well as the assurance that Someone is helping us to transcend our own frailty and limitation. For ethical conduct can no longer be concerned with merely keeping rules. It must involve a sense of responsibility for the whole material world, just as religion must now direct itself not toward observances but toward that which makes any observance at all worth while, namely our ability to live in the world and before God in a fully human way. Hence in Teilhard's evolutionary system of thought the significance of Christianity for the present shift in human consciousness is that it offers hope that such change is in fact good, in both its inception and its outcome, and that it will indeed, if followed to its completion, succeed in making men and women more fully human. I think it will be worth our while, in this opening chapter, to spell out this significance in some detail.

I

Before we see what Teilhard has to contribute to our under-standing of the current crisis, let us take a closer look at the crisis itself. Erik Erikson has characterized it quite simply as one of identity. "The traditional sources of identity strength—economic, racial, national, religious, occupational—are all in the process of allying themselves with a new world-image in which the vision of an anticipated future and, in fact, of a future in a permanent state of planning will take over much of the power of tradition."[4] Erikson sees two principal ideological orientations as basic to the formation of future identities, the technological and the humanist, and even the great politico-economic alternatives will, he be-lieves, be subordinated to these. The cultural conditioning along technological and scientific lines has already been taking place for some time, according to Erikson, but is being opposed more and more by a humanist orientation, which insists that beyond the technological there is a much wider range of human values and possibilities now in danger of being lost. The technologists and the humanists seem to live in separate ecologies and almost to belong to different species: they oppose and repel each other; the acceptance of even part of one orientation could result in an ideological slide in the other's whole cluster of images, aspira-tions, hopes, fears, and hates. Erikson sees this polarity to be most important in fostering a dynamic interplay between the techno-logical and humanist identity, leading, he is convinced, to radically new modes of thought and daring innovations in both culture and society. But he makes a point of adding to this judgment an ominous condition: "provided we survive."

This question of survival in fact hovers in the background of most discussions of the present crisis, whether described as one of identity or otherwise. Among the young there is the growing fear that, in spite of what their elders say about progress, mankind has no future to look forward to at all. Psychiatrists have argued that there is serious psychoanalytic evidence for saying that people today are suffering from an unconscious despair lurking just under the surface of their lives, a despair arising on the one hand from fear of becoming an appendage to the machine, and on the other from the sense of having less and less to say about their own destiny.[5] Beneath this unrest is a deep and well-justified fear: that the next step in technological progress may bring about the annihilation of man. In *Beyond,* I. A. Richards recognizes with great reluctance that we face within thirty years the imminent collapse of the human effort. The Vietnam war disturbed so many because they saw the atrocious methods of conducting American military operations not only as a threat against their own existence, but as an ominous prelude to the whole future. In their unconscious, says Lewis Mumford, many are living in a postcatastrophic world, and their conduct is rational in terms of that world. They see survival as problematic precisely because we do not seem able to control the technology we have created, and because the technological society we *thought* we were making is not being made at all.

Not long ago this despair of survival was greatly fostered by a best seller entitled *Chance and Necessity,* written by Jacques Monod, winner of the 1965 Nobel Prize in medicine for his studies in genetics. His avowed task in the book is to sweep the slate clean of virtually all previous philosophies of life. He locates our present crisis in the fact that we are using the wealth of modern science to practice and teach systems of values which that very science has already destroyed at the roots. He wants to show, he says, that there is no harmony whatsoever between man and his world, that man himself is a freak, a product of pure chance, a quite accidental mutation in that otherwise fixed and invariable microscopic machine known as the genetic code. "If he accepts this message—accepts all it contains—then man must at last wake out of his millenary dream; and in doing so, wake to his total solitude, his fundamental isolation. Now does he at last realize that, like a gypsy, he lives on the boundary of an alien world. A world that is deaf to his music, just as indifferent to his hopes as it is to his suffering or his crimes."[6] Like Albert Camus, who he admits influenced him greatly, Dr. Monod sees man faced with the utterly meaningless task of Sisyphus endlessly pushing his stone up the mountain only to have it roll back down again. Yet though he believes with Camus that "the struggle toward the summit is itself enough to fill the heart of man," he wonders nonetheless whether man will actually continue this struggle in the future. "There is absolutely no doubt," he concludes, "that the risk of the race committing suicide is very great. In my opinion the future of mankind is going to be decided within the next two generations." Completely alone in a fundamentally unreliable and hostile world-process, man must now choose whether to move forward or to stop.[7]

While Monod's analysis is admittedly a pessimistic extreme, it nonetheless highlights the crossroads at which the human race finds itself, as well as the two paradoxical poles of estrangement and participation which we encounter everywhere in society. Gibson Winter puts his finger on the nerve center of this divided consciousness when he remarks that it "arises from a sense of belonging together and yet thinking of ourselves as isolated individuals called upon to make our way by private initiative."[8] The tight web of interdependence created by technology thus tends to produce greater alienation and estrangement, since the desire to participate is not yet strong enough to accept the new social reality before us. "We are witnessing," continues Winter, "a communal movement of national and even global scope. The participating consciousness is accompanied by a profound search for a new sensibility," of which drugs and rock festivals are only symptoms.[9] The crucial question, however, is whether this humanizing tendency will triumph, whether participation will indeed emerge as the creative principle in converting the oppressive society into a liberated humanity. For always present is the temptation to sacrifice the individual to collectivity, as well as that all-important third factor in the crisis, namely, despair of survival.

It is interesting to compare the diagnoses we have been discussing with that made by Teilhard de Chardin over thirty years ago. "O man of the twentieth century," he asked, "how does it happen that you are waking up to horizons and are susceptible to fears that your forefathers never knew? . . . Here at this turning point where the future substitutes itself for the present . . . do our perplexities inevitably begin. Tomorrow? But who can guarantee us a tomorrow anyway? And without this assurance that tomorrow exists, can we really go on living, we to whom has been given the terrible gift of foresight? Sickness of the dead end. . . . This time we have at last put our finger on the tender spot."[10] It is this tender spot—the growing suspicion that he has nowhere to go in the universe—that causes modern man to ask whether or not he has been duped by life. An animal may rush headlong down a blind alley or toward a precipice, but a human being, precisely because he can *reflect* upon his condition, will no longer continue to take steps in a direction he knows to be blocked. In spite of our control of material energy, in spite of the pressures of immediate needs and desires, without a taste for life people will simply stop inventing and constructing. The species, in other words, is quite capable of going on strike. Indeed, it will surely do so unless, as Teilhard says, "we should be assured the space and the chances to fulfill ourselves, that is to say, to progress till we arrive (directly or indirectly, individually or collectively) at the utmost limits of ourselves."[11]

Here we face the crucial question. Where is such an assurance to come from? How shall we be liberated from the fear that this struggle between individual and collectivity, between personal and technological, is a hopeless one which will destroy us? Teilhard's answer is that assurance must come first of all from man himself, from his own experience of being part of an evolutionary movement which has come from prelife to life and then to man himself. "To bring us into existence it has from the beginning juggled with too many improbabilities for there to be any risk whatever in committing ourselves further and following it right to the end. . . . Life, by its very structure, having once been lifted to its stage of thought, cannot go on at all without ascending higher."[12] But Teilhard always believed that people need and indeed seek assurance on a much deeper level than their experience of the world around them. The level, in other words, of religious experience—of their awareness of a divine presence and initiative in the world. For Teilhard this divine presence was concretized in the Person of Jesus Christ, so much so that he could say: "Christ comes to modern man . . . not only to save him from legitimate revolt against a life with the least threat or suspicion of total death, but also to bring him the greatest possible stimulus, without which living thought on our planet could surely never reach its destiny."[13] With this background, let us examine in turn the two assurances of Teilhard, the one from man, the other from Christ.

II

Teilhard's whole system of thought can be characterized, I think, as an effort to explain to contemporary man that what is happening to him in the twentieth century is intelligible and, even more importantly, capable of success. The intelligibility Teilhard proposes depends, of course, upon his understanding of evolution, which he saw to be not simply change but directional change; not simply development, but development with a purpose. Hence his description of the process as "genesis," from the French word *genèse,* which can be applied to any form of production involving successive stages and oriented toward some goal. In the case of evolution, or cosmogenesis, this goal is the human species. Far from being an exception to biological evolution, we have here in reality the key to the entire process, precisely because the phenomenon of thought, or reflective consciousness, comes at the end of a progressive interiorization of matter over millions of years and represents "a mutation from zero to everything."[14] From this point onward the evolutionary process continues its development not so much in the sphere of life as in the sphere of mind and spirit, the noosphere, and this particular type of genesis is best described not as cosmogenesis but as noogenesis. Thus "the social phenomenon is the culmination and not the attenuation of the biological phenomenon."[15]

At this point, however, Teilhard makes a most unusual analysis of that directional change in human history which he calls noogenesis. Let us imagine, he says, using the geometrical image of meridians on a globe, that a pulsation enters a sphere at its south pole and spreads out on the surface of the sphere in the direction of the north pole. The movement of this wave is a converging one from the start, since it is on a curved surface, but it has two very different phases: one of expansion from the south pole to the equator and the other of contraction from the equator to the north pole. Now no better image illustrates the crisis of growth through which humanity is passing at this very moment. In the first millions of years of its existence it has been expanding more or less freely, slowly covering more and more of the uninhabited earth. Because lack of space was no problem, the result was that century after century the socializing process was also extremely slow. There was a gradual branching out into the various races; civilizations were able to grow and rub shoulders on a sparsely inhabited planet without encountering any major difficulty. "But now," says Teilhard, "following the dramatic growth of industry, communications and populations in the course of a single century, we can discern the outline of a formidable event. The hitherto scattered fragments of humanity, being at length brought into close contact, are beginning to interpenetrate to the point of reacting economically and psychically upon each other."[16] Given the fundamental relationship between geographic compression and the heightening of consciousness, the result is an irresistible rise within and around us of the level of reflection.

In other words, what we have been experiencing for some time now, without being aware of it, is in reality the beginning of the second phase of noogenesis, that of contraction. In our own time the human race has crossed the equatorial point and entered into a new stage in the development of the species.

> From the first beginnings of history [wrote Teilhard in 1950] this principle of the compressive generation of consciousness has been ceaselessly at work in the human mass. But from the moment—we have just reached it!—when the compression of populations in the teeming continents gains a decided ascendancy over their movement of expansion upon the earth's surface, the process is speeded up to a staggering extent. We are today witnessing a truly explosive growth of technology and research, bringing an increasing mastery, both theoretical and practical, of the secrets and sources of cosmic energy at every level and in every form; and, correlative with this, the rapid heightening of what I have called the psychic temperature of the earth. A single glance at the overall picture of surface chaos is enough to assure us that this is so.[17]

Teilhard, however, was not only concerned to explain our modern anxiety and so make it intelligible; he also wanted to assuage it by showing us that what was taking place in and through our developing consciousness was indeed capable of success. This he does, first of all, by locating today's existential fear in our sudden realization that we are now in control of the evolutionary process. Through us evolution has not only become conscious of itself but free to dispose of itself. Until the mid-twentieth century the vast majority of people were like passengers closed up in the hold of a ship distracting themselves as did the men in Plato's cave. When more and more of them climbed up to the bridge, however, they gradually became aware not only of the drift of the universe, but also of the risks and dangers in guiding the ship. To use Teilhard's phrase, the task before them now is "to seize the tiller of the world," to take hold of the energies by which man has reached his present position and use them to move ahead.[18] But this is a fearful task, and to counteract our awesome power to refuse it, we must cultivate our moral sense of obligation to life. If we do not, then we face either ecological disaster or nuclear destruction. Thus the fundamental law of morality for Teilhard is to liberate that conscious energy which seeks further to unify the world. This energy is what he calls "the zest for life," that disposition of mind and heart that savors the experience of life, manifesting itself particularly in the relish a person has for creative tasks undertaken from a sense of duty.

> Such a man would see the greatness of his responsibilities increasing almost to infinity before him. Hitherto he could think of himself in nature as a bird of passage, local, accidental, free to waste the spark of life that is given him, with no loss to anyone but himself. Suddenly he finds in his heart the fearful task of conserving, increasing and transmitting the fortunes of a whole world. His life, in a true sense, has ceased to be private to him. Body and soul, he is the product of a huge creative work with which the totality of things has collaborated from the beginning; if he refuses the task assigned to him, some part of that effort will be lost forever and lacking throughout the whole future. . . . For the briefest moment the success of the whole affair, of this huge universal childbirth, actually rests in the hands of the least among us.[19]

This effort of Teilhard to show that what is taking place in men and women is indeed capable of success had to deal eventually with a fear much stronger than the fear of freedom: namely, the fear of collectivity. For nothing is more terrifying today than the specter of the mechanized, impersonal world of George Orwell's *1984,* a vast technological complex blind to the needs and values of individuals. Yet when we look into the future what we see is precisely this social destiny, quite capable of stifling the personality rather than developing it. In Teilhard's mind this is the reason for the world's present discouragement with any human aspiration toward unity. Every effort to unify man seems to end by stifling the human person. What people forget, says Teilhard, is that—monstrous though it is—modern totalitarianism is really a distortion of something magnificent, a unifying energy based not upon coercion or fear but upon love. Love is the only energy in the world that is capable of personalizing by totalizing, of promoting synthesis without destroying the person. It alone unites human beings in such a way as to complete and fulfill them. And the reason is that "in any domain—whether it be the cells of a body, the members of a society or the elements of a spiritual synthesis —*union differentiates.* In every organized whole the parts perfect themselves and fulfill themselves."[20] This familiar evolutionary pattern of differentiating union is thus applied by Teilhard to the personalizing union of beings who relate to each other as persons. In this way "the grains of consciousness do not tend to lose their outlines and blend, but, on the contrary, to accentuate the depth and incommunicability of their *egos.* The more 'other' they become in conjunction, the more they find themselves as 'self.' "[21]

Hence the importance of the concept of "amorization" in Teilhard's work, which is the gradual release of the power of love, the response of truly free men and women to increased social pressure. Only love can turn increasing socialization from a threat to a promise. Human beings need not fear the contemporary drift toward unity as long as they can freely relate to each other through what is most intimate to themselves. This fostering of freedom through love is the one way to counteract the blind necessity that forces us to actualize technological achievement simply because we *can* do so. The question of whether we *should* do so must be asked, and asked in the context of the primacy of the person and the need for more humane ways to manage change. It is thus through amorization, or the growth of love, that humankind can cope with the tendency to turn in upon itself in individual isolation and allow the world to become more and more mechanized and impersonal. "Considered in its full biological reality," concludes Teilhard, "love—that is to say the affinity of being with being—is not peculiar to man. . . . If there were no internal propensity to unite, even at a prodigiously elementary level—indeed in the molecule itself—it would be physically impossible for love to appear higher up, with us, in 'hominized' form. . . . Love in all its subtleties is nothing more, and nothing less, than the more or less direct trace marked on the heart of the element by the psychical convergence of the universe upon itself."[22]

III

Our focus up to now has been upon the modern need to be liberated from the fear of a hopeless and destructive struggle between individual and collectivity. I have presented at some length the answer which Teilhard de Chardin found in man himself: that the present crisis of consciousness is a turning point in the whole evolutionary process, whose movement toward greater socialization can be successfully personalized by the free and conscious release of love energy. Teilhard never hesitated for a moment to admit that this analysis of man's chances of success is based upon an act of faith. Neither on the side of pessimism nor on the side of optimism, he wrote, "is there any tangible evidence to produce. Only, in support of hope, there are rational invitations to an act of faith."[23] Yet Teilhard was well aware that these rational invitations, however strong, were not enough either for him or for others. For the essence of the scientific and technological mind, as Barrington Moore has pointed out, is largely the refusal to believe on the basis of hope. Such belief therefore always remains fragile and insecure, and what Teilhard sought above all was an assurance that would be grounded upon some absolute. Hence his eagerness to give to the contemporary change in consciousness a religious dimension. What he does now is to point to the meaning which Christianity, and Christianity alone, gives to the two phenomena most involved in this change of consciousness: namely, death and love.

"The radical defect of all forms of belief in progress," he once wrote, "is that they do not definitely eliminate death. What is the use of detecting a focus of any sort in the van of evolution if that focus can and must one day disintegrate?"[24] It is psychologically impossible, Teilhard believed, for human beings to take part very long in the struggle of life unless the best of their achievements are preserved from total destruction. For a primary attribute of human consciousness today is precisely the will to survive. Applied to the individual, the idea of total extinction may not at first sight appal us; but extended to humanity as a whole it revolts and sickens. The fact is that the more humanity becomes aware of its duration and the enormous burden it must bear in order to survive, the more it realizes that if all this labor is to end in nothing, then we have really been cheated and should indeed rebel. The new consciousness must therefore face the need of assurance in regard to some ultimate conquest of death. Can it really accept a total death, an unscalable wall against which it would crash and then forever disappear? And can this really be reconciled with the mechanism of reflection without that mechanism breaking its mainspring? It is here, Teilhard concludes, "in its proper place in terms of science, that we come to the problem of God."[25]

More specifically, we come to the Christian phenomenon and the message it proclaims to the world that the true meaning of death is the passage to new life in and through Christ. "We shall find the Christian faith absolutely explicit in what it affirms and practices. Christ has conquered death not only by suppressing its evil effects but by reversing its sting. Through the power of the resurrection nothing any longer kills inevitably. . . . The great victory of the Creator and Redeemer, in the Christian vision, is to have transformed what is itself a universal power of diminishment and extinction into an essentially life-giving factor."[26] Such transformation, moreover, takes place precisely in and through matter, and this is why Teilhard can speak of what he calls the "hominization of death." Just as a current causes a ship to deviate from its course, so the cosmic influence of Christ is responsible for the general "drift" of matter toward spirit. The positive meaning of the Christian doctrine of redemption is, according to Teilhard, the support given by Christ's suffering, death, and resurrection to the upward movement of man in the noosphere. Christ gives this support because through his incarnation he has achieved in his own Body-Person the purpose of the whole evolutionary process, namely the union of humanity with God in and through a purification of matter. The world is therefore above all a work of creation continued in Christ, and Christ saves the world in the sense that without him human effort would be without any ultimate hope of success, and this would mean that people would inevitably lose their taste for life and abandon altogether their task on earth.[27]

This significance for modern consciousness of Christian hope in the victory of life over death naturally leads Teilhard to underline the relationship between faith in the risen Christ and the phenomenon of human love. It is of capital importance, he writes, "that on an appreciable region of the earth there has appeared and grown a zone of thought in which a genuine universal love has not only been conceived and preached, but has also been shown to be psychologically possible and operative in practice. It is all the more capital inasmuch as, far from decreasing, the movement seems to wish to gain still greater speed and intensity."[28] The historian of religion who measures the movement of Christianity not by quantitative expansion but by the qualitative evolution of an act of love immediately finds himself tracing the curve of a true progress. For since the time of Christ, the theory and practice of total love have never ceased to become more precise and to be transmitted in ever wider circles. "The result is that, after a spiritual experience of two thousand years, our capacity for union with the personal Center of the universe has grown as much in the richness of its power to express itself as has our capacity for union with the natural spheres of the world after two thousand years of science."[29] What modern man needs, according to Teilhard, is to find the source of a truly universal love, for only this will conquer his "dread of that frightful cosmic machinery in which he finds himself entangled." The enthusiasm engendered by naturalistic humanisms eventually becomes cold, joyless, and hard. Christianity alone can teach man "not only how to serve (which is not enough) but how to love deeply, in all its manifestations . . . a universe whose very evolution has been impregnated with love."[30]

It should be noted at this point that although Teilhard believed strongly in the power of Christ to activate the love energy of the world, he in no way minimized either the risk of human freedom or the frailty of human love. Indeed, it is because the risk is great and this frailty perennial that ambiguity will always characterize human progress. Essentially, says Teilhard, "progress is a force and the most dangerous of forces. . . . Progress is directed toward fostering in the human will reflective action and fully human choice."[31] Noogenesis is thus a movement endangered from within. For the collective growth it fosters in man's capacity for reflection, love, and global unity is precisely a growth in *capacity* —not in love itself. And with growth in the power to love comes also growth in the power to refuse love. The prospect must therefore be faced that the universal love of Christ will ultimately give life and fulfillment to a fraction only of the noosphere. There may well be what Teilhard calls "an internal schism of consciousness," divided on two opposite ideals of evolution, and in this case the positive attraction of Christ would be exerted only upon the hearts of those who turn toward him. In any case, he says, "there is not to be indefinite progress, which is an hypothesis contrary to the converging nature of noogenesis, but an ecstasy transcending the dimensions and framework of the visible universe. Ecstasy in concord or discord; but in either case by excess of interior tension: the only biological outcome proper to or conceivable for the phenomenon of man."[32]

IV

I have been attempting in this chapter to sketch in briefest outline the significance of Pierre Teilhard de Chardin for the change taking place today in the consciousness of man. Long before recent diagnoses, Teilhard located the crisis of change in a loss of nerve. For large numbers the arrival of the future has been accelerated to an alarming degree, and growing technological control appears to be either an invitation to self-destruction or a headlong return to the regimentation of the anthill. Does the human being as such really have nowhere to go? Is life really so absurd that the values of the individual person, his desire for community, interpersonal creativity, and the preservation of the world of nature around him can no longer be fostered after so many centuries of growth? Teilhard insists that all this fear of survival is at its root a fear of total death for the species, and that if there is no assurance of life to be had, then the human enterprise is surely pointless and what happens to us wholly irrelevant. But an assurance of life *does* exist, and it resides first of all in the enormous capacity of human love to bring individuals, and indeed the whole species, closer and closer together in more complex social structures without injuring what is most personal and intimate. For love fosters freedom and expansion, not repression or diminishment. Human love, however, in spite of its capacity to unite without depersonalizing, cannot motivate the race without further assurance, for each of us is aware of the frailty of our love. Unless some divine power strengthens human love and supports human freedom, the ultimate success of noogenesis will forever remain doubtful and insecure. As a Christian, Teilhard saw this ultimate source of love in the Person of Christ, who by his incarnation, death, and resurrection has conquered the native human tendency toward repulsion and isolation. For only what God has done in Christ brings assurance that human creativity is indeed a participation in God's creativity, and that the outcome will therefore be on the side of life and not on the side of death.

Nevertheless, we must recognize that Teilhard's hope was not clear. In Christianity he saw rational invitations to an act of faith in the future. His whole life was an affirmation of that faith in spite of all the discouragement that came from human failure and stupidity. "It is a terrifying thing to have been born," he wrote once. "I mean to find oneself, without having willed it, swept irrevocably along a torment of fearful energy which seems as though it wished to destroy everything it carries with it."[33] The terror experienced by people today as they take responsibility for the future was experienced by Teilhard himself. Through Christ, however, he saw that a new impulse of hope was possible and was now beginning to take shape in human consciousness. This hope was that the time-space totality of evolution would be immortalized and personalized in Christ to the extent that it would become lovable. This is why he could pray: "What I want, my God, is that by a reversal of forces which you alone can bring about, my terror in the face of nameless changes of renewal may be turned into an overflowing joy at being transformed into you."[34] Like all men whose hope is strong, Teilhard cherished every sign of new life and was ready at any moment to help the birth of what is ready to be born. Yet he was a man who hoped in the midst of doubt —doubt which, like human suffering, he recognized as the price and condition for the perfection of the universe. And under these conditions he was content to walk right to the end along a road of which he was more and more certain, toward an horizon more and more shrouded in mist.

2

Conflict

In his new book, *The Survival of the Wisest,* Jonas Salk advances the thesis that the human race is now attempting to master the process of transition from what he calls an "Epoch A" society, characterized by win-lose strategies, to a new civilization, "Epoch B," in which its values must be manifestly different. Our task in this transition is to grow in wisdom, by which Salk means the ability to live in harmony with nature, of which we are part, and with ourselves. In the past man's struggle for survival pitted him against nature, but now it seems to be taking place within himself. The results of this struggle, Salk says, are wholly unpredictable, and for this reason he compares the behavior of the human species to that of a cancer: cancerous cells escape organismic control, give no warning of future behavior, and inevitably commit suicide by destroying the maintenance systems upon which they depend. Unlike such cells, however, the human being is acknowledged to be trustee of his own maintenance system. Nature's task is to proceed, ours is to understand and direct, since we alone in nature can reflect upon and be conscious of ourselves. We possess what Salk calls an enormous anticipatory potential, which enables us to respond quickly to new circumstances at all levels of life. The present situation is therefore aptly expressed by the Chinese ideogram for "crisis," made up of the two symbols for "danger" and "opportunity." For all life, especially human life, is error-correcting as well as error-making; to prevent all errors the whole process would have to stop.[1]

This question of error, however, is all-important and is directly responsible for that loss of nerve of which I spoke in the first chapter. What makes us afraid is that our key decisions deal with so many peoples and nations that the number of mistakes we can afford is diminishing rapidly. Is this not to inhibit or even paralyze the error-correcting process? Like the ancient apocalyptic, the modern mood is one of radical disorientation, in which "there are not only no answers; there are no categories, no questions."[2] Obviously Christian faith has to rethink itself in terms of this contemporary experience. William Beardslee has underlined the fact that faith is always formed by a given culture, even when it criticizes it, and unless faith and culture are to be forced into separate worlds of their own, some way has to be found for them both to speak to the same reality. Since the basic Christian insight is the stance of receiving life as a gift, it is not impossible to see a connection between Christianity and man's basic biological tendency toward growth and self-preservation.[3] The question is where and how such a connection is to be made. How is the Christian sense that the future is ultimately trustworthy to be related to man's contemporary sense of responsibility for his destiny?

What I will argue for in what follows is that the point of contact is an exploration of the unfinished character of the human creature, which has only now begun to preoccupy the biological and social sciences as well as theology and art. At the risk of oversimplification let us focus upon this phenomenon from three distinct points of view: our peculiar capacity to dream of societies better than our own; the conflict between peoples which must inevitably come as soon as such dreams begin to be realized; finally, the effort of religious man, especially Christian man, to make sense of his faith in the light of such conflict and dreams.

I

It has been pointed out often enough that, on the scale of an evolution which could continue for millions of years, *homo sapiens sapiens* is a very young species. Only a few thousand years have passed since the human race began taking initiatives in the world, and in spite of an accelerated cultural development it is still in its childhood. Only recently, however, have the full implications of this fact begun to manifest themselves. Dostoevsky's legend of the Grand Inquisitor, for example, takes on new significance. Christ returns to the scene of the Spanish Inquisition and is accused of offering to man gifts he is incapable of accepting. Man cannot live with riches such as freedom and love, the Inquisitor says, but can be happy only with authority and bread. Freedom and responsibility are burdens too heavy to bear. John O'Manique has suggested that this judgment on man's condition may indeed have been true until now, and notes that many social critics today see the Inquisitor in the form of advanced technological society which seeks to bestow upon us whatever will satisfy our appetites and deepen our sense of security.[4] B. F. Skinner's insistence that man's freedom as well as his dignity are both illusions would seem to provide added confirmation.[5] If all human action can be explained either by genetic makeup or social conditioning, then we can improve the species whenever we wish simply by altering environmental controls. Instead of an Inquisitor we shall have a controlling elite of psychologists whose function is to provide bread to keep our bodies content while not in the least agitating the spirit.

Obviously no one would deny that we are to some extent both genetically and socially conditioned, as is every other animal species. The question is to what extent people have tended historically to react in a peculiarly *human* way to such conditioning, either rejecting it or interiorizing it self-consciously. Moreover, whatever may be one's judgment on the past, current responses by both individual and species would clearly disappoint the Inquisitor. For there is growing awareness today of the degree to which everyone has come to depend upon everyone else; the histories of all peoples are now seen to be parts of a single history. Technology itself, which might seem at first to be the new instrument for controlling society and reducing its freedom, is actually becoming the instrument for transforming the world into the raw material for responsible human activity. Such rational reflection is even being applied to the changing of humanity itself through population limitation and genetic engineering. "The subject is becoming its own most proper object; man is becoming his own creator."[6] There is thus every reason to believe that we humans of the unified planet, interlaced with networks of instant communication, are really still standing at the beginning of our history. For we seem about to embark upon a journey to qualitatively new ways of being human, which will show for the first time what we really are. We are aware that we can, if we wish, create a society qualitatively different from our own, which may in fact be hundreds or even thousands of years hence, but which will be the result of an energy peculiar to ourselves and rooted in our freedom of choice.

More accurately, perhaps, such newness is rooted in the power of imagination. Jean Monnet once said, in speaking of the unity of Europe, that in order for any great human undertaking to succeed there must always be a certain dream-element. But if it lasts, the dream one day becomes reality, because we apply ourselves to overcoming the difficulties necessary for its achievement. Gradually the dream fades away and its accomplishment appears. These dreams of the species are the stuff of imagination, and our unfinished character appears precisely in their unremitting newness. They extend the power of our will to effect change by constantly relating past memory and future intention to present concentration and choice.[7] Hence the significance of novelty in history: not the development of potentialities preexistent in humanity, but rather the human being's ever present capacity to seize control of himself and the things of life and, if he so desires, to make both them and himself anew. This is what is taking place now. Whoever counters current dreams of the future with skepticism or scorn for "impossible utopias" has presumably experienced none of the hunger or restlessness abroad today, none of the discontent or sense that we must somehow make a new start in our social and global relations, and do so quickly. "Little by little a more universal form of human culture is developing," said the Second Vatican Council. "In every group or nation there is an ever increasing number of men and women who are conscious that they themselves are the artisans and the authors of the culture of their community. . . . Such a development is of paramount importance for the spiritual and moral maturity of the human race. . . . We are witnesses of the birth of a new humanism, one in which man is defined first of all by his responsibility toward his brothers and toward history."[8]

This apparently perennial ability to imagine new and better societies is a good indication that the future is really an inner moment of our actual being. Prognosis, in other words, is necessary for humans as human. They need to forecast and project for their own self-understanding, since what they come to know in this way is the futurity of their present self. The real subject of the future is thus that part of the individual which will still be real at the time a particular future becomes present. There must consequently be an element in the human person which cannot be reduced to the temporal. Otherwise, if there were no such absolute value to man as a person, if he were totally contingent and time-bound, why should anyone living today dedicate himself to shaping tomorrow for men and women equally contingent and time-bound? Surely the question of *my* existence is not solved by saying that it will be solved for people generations hence. Yet it is with these people still unborn that dreams of a better future are concerned, and not simply with the use of technology, statistics, and sociological guesswork. Persons therefore somehow transcend the boundaries of their consciousness, and in and through this transcendence their futures somehow become present.[9]

No one, moreover, dedicates himself to realizing a dream of the future without making at least an implicit value judgment on what it means to be human. A good case has been made, for example, for the belief that people as we know them in our harshly competitive society are a distortion and not truly human at all. What the human creature has to work at is finding the way to its true self—being remade, as it were, into its original likeness. This obviously involves an option that human nature is basically worthy of trust and that rationality is more fundamental to it than chaos. In this context John Macquarrie has pointed to the contrast between the biblical notion of peace as *shalom,* a positive quality of individual and social life, and the Roman notion of *pax,* understood as a mere cessation of strife, an artificial construct designed to lessen the misery of unremitting conflict. In the first case conflict is not seen to be a primary given in the human character, but a falling away from one's true self through sin. Nor was *shalom* conceived as a permanent state or condition, but rather as a process, a task of moving from potentiality to realization. For man's nature has over the centuries become so perverted by hostility that peace can only be established through a costly *metanoia.* Obviously there is no conclusive empirical evidence to prove that the peace we seek is really *shalom* and not *pax*—that we are by nature rational and sociable rather than hostile and mean. "But even to hold one or other of these views," says Macquarrie, "tends to bring about the state of affairs it envisages. In each case the first alternative promotes an attitude of trust which prevents the break-down of communication . . . while the second alternative undermines trust and fosters fear and alienation."[10] Hence to dream of a world at peace in the sense of *shalom* is to dream of giving free course to a wholeness that is already part of the gift of being human. Woodrow Wilson was a statesman who shared such a dream, but when he asked Georges Clemenceau whether he too believed in the brotherhood of man, the latter replied: "Yes, I believe in the brotherhood of man. Cain and Abel!"[11]

II

We have been focusing up to now upon the unfinished character of human nature from the viewpoint of imagination. This extraordinary power to dream of changing ourselves for the better has, in this century, begun to be operative for whole peoples, conscious for the first time that their lives and their world are objects for free and responsible action. The judgment of Dostoevsky's Inquisitor may have been accurate in a former age; it is much less so today, and it may be totally false tomorrow. This change does not involve, it should be noted, any utopian belief in the possibility of a perfect society, but rather recognition that, since all societies are imperfect, no particular one is necessary. A realistic imagination does not dream of abolishing human frailty and malice, but rather of abolishing one mode of being human and creating another, whether this involves structures in a given society or certain styles of human behavior. For what is now coming to characterize the human species is a growing consciousness that historical realities exist because men and women in the past built them, and that they can be replaced whenever a sufficient number of people decide to create new ones. Man the dreamer is free to actualize his dream. To say that he is not is to deny that he transcends his environment. To say that he *should* not is to focus upon the second aspect of his unfinished character, namely that in any given society people have to struggle with other people to achieve their dreams.

This aspect of struggle and conflict between persons and groups of different value judgments has always been part of any change in social structures. Freud attributed such conflict to the fact that the human social animal is by the same token the neurotic animal; our capacity for neurosis is merely the obverse of our capacity for cultural development. Neurosis is thus an essential consequence of civilization and culture. For Freud the essence of the human being consists not so much in thinking, as Descartes maintained, but in desiring: only a wish, he says, can possibly set our psychic apparatus in motion. Yet reality frustrates desire, and this conflict is the cause of repression and therefore of neurosis. On the other hand, neurotic symptoms show that the frustrations of reality cannot destroy these desires: we still hold fast to a deep-rooted and passionate striving for their fulfillment. Christianity has always recognized this human restlessness and discontent, though it sees its ultimate origin inside ourselves to be not repressed unconscious desires but the presence of God. In moving toward his final destiny with God, said Augustine, man is always in tension with himself, driven by two loves, true love on the one hand and the lust for power on the other. Freud saw this desire for power as ultimately a flight from death, and identified aggression as an extroversion of the death instinct. "This extroversion of the death instinct," comments Norman O. Brown, "is the peculiar human solution to a peculiar human problem. It is the flight from death that leaves mankind with the problem of what to do with its own innate biological dying, what to do with its own repressed death. Animals let death be a part of life, and use the death instinct to die: man aggressively builds immortal structures and makes history in order to fight death."[12]

Whether or not one agrees with Freud's interpretation, struggle must necessarily be part of whatever improvement in life we dream of achieving. The reason is quite simply that the *status quo* at any given time will always be defended and maintained against anyone able to free himself from the grip of dominant values and anticipate requirements of the future. The movement of history is never smooth. Change and development occur precisely in and through moments of rupture when enough men and women take a qualitative leap in consciousness. While this is obviously true of a violent disruption like revolution, it is just as true of the energetic but less acute type of disruption which is becoming more and more common in the twentieth century. I take this to be Hannah Arendt's meaning when she says that to understand revolution may be the only way to understand the future of human society.[13] In any case, political and economic equality in their various forms always have to be won by the many from the few. Those who hold power rarely if ever give it up except under pressure of some kind. This pressure in turn represents an historical initiative on behalf of new egalitarian structures or new approaches to freedom and opportunity. The reason such initiatives are always directed against social, political, or economic structures is that these play an essential part in the explanation of injustice in the world. The simple moral conversion of individuals rarely affects such structures and therefore does relatively little to create new futures. These futures depend upon initiatives in the public forum, which will always be opposed by those who believe that the only desirable change is some improved version of the present.

This phenomenon of conflict between those who dream of different futures is well illustrated by current liberation movements in Latin America and elsewhere. The point at issue is, of course, the obvious inequities between the rich nations and the poor nations, as well as the future self-determination of Third World countries. Until the 1960's underdeveloped areas were confident that they would eventually develop by imitating the economic processes of more developed societies. They accepted the fact that they were in some prior stage of these processes and therefore obliged to go through more or less the same historical experiences as those of the wealthier nations in order to reach equal status. This is still the opinion of many serious thinkers in Europe and North America who advocate continued and uncontrolled growth for international business. It is this type of institution, they argue, that contains the true economic and technical potential for the Third World, since the large transnational corporation is alone able effectively to innovate development on a scale large enough to achieve for the poor new levels and quality of life. The Industrial Revolution shows this. It took place in Europe and America because a certain cultural climate enabled these peoples to develop the necessary technological, scientific, and entrepreneurial spirit. For comparable results these "Western" attitudes and values need only be imitated, as in the case of Japan, since they can now be transported and taught rapidly to any people in the world. Hence—according to this view—the real political problem in Third World countries arises not from economics but from politics, from efforts of national states locally to control international business and prevent the inflow of information and advanced technique. This goal then results in theories which condemn all developed economies as exploitative, as well as inimical to any given nation's cultural and spiritual values.[14]

The proponents of liberation have come to reject this view of development because they now believe it to be merely a cloak for perpetuating the oppressive dependence of the poor upon the rich. They see the underdevelopment of some countries as the historical subproduct of development in others: over the last decade the dynamics of capitalistic economies have at one and the same time led to greater wealth for fewer and to greater poverty for more. Between 5 and 10 percent of the population of Latin America now control over half its wealth; half the people of the world have a per capita income of under $100 a year; in 1970 the *increase* of the gross national product of the United States was equal to the *entire* gross national product of Africa, giving Americans more for luxuries than Africans had for everything. The poor of the world now know all this and know, too, that it need not be so. They are angry at what they see to be the injustice of the entire economic order. Financial and other aid offered by rich nations is thus viewed with the greatest suspicion. Could these nations possibly support programs which would jeopardize their economic superiority? Is such aid not rather designed to keep the poor in submission and to foster a paternalistic relationship between donor and recipient? And is it not usually given in greatest measure to totalitarian governments which immediately repress whatever might threaten these foreign investments?[15]

The conflict pattern I have just sketched is obviously a confrontation between two totally different perceptions of what human beings are doing with their world and what their future should be like: the one based upon an experience of affluence, technological progress, and generosity to the needy, and the other upon the very opposite experience of indigence, technological oppression, and economic exploitation. Unfortunately most people of the rich nations know almost nothing of the dehumanizing life of the world's poor and so are vastly puzzled at the latter's present efforts to denounce and repudiate those structures of society in which they feel themselves trapped. Hence the immediate source of conflict is not the validity of one economic theory or the other but the actual experience by vast numbers of men and women in the Third World of what has been called "institutionalized violence," by which is meant a society so organized in favor of the privileged class that the masses are forced to live in an inhuman condition. Paulo Freire has called such awareness "conscientization," the process "of learning to perceive social, political, and economic contradictions and to take action against the oppressive elements of reality."[16] In the end such action is less protest than aspiration, the dream of a qualitatively different society capable of freeing the illiterate from that stupefying fatalism which has characterized and inhibited them in the past. Such dreams are now emerging with renewed energy among the populace of the poor nations and show every sign of getting stronger rather than weaker. If the social change needed to achieve at least some of them does not take place rapidly enough by nonviolent means, then these peoples seem more and more ready to use violence.

There are those who fear that the tendency of present liberation movements is to alienate so deeply that a far more intense and hopeless sense of oppression results than is now actually experienced. Although this is a very serious question, we cannot deal with it here. Nor is it to our purpose to ask about the uses of power in its various forms. The point I am making is simply the inevitability of conflict, given the unfinished character of the human creature and the fact that different value judgments can be made upon its future development. As long as all those making such contrary judgments possess power, this conflict can still be creative. For power gives freedom to initiate action and anticipate change, and so provides a basis of human dignity. Only when the power of one side is in jeopardy is violence likely to appear, since, as Hannah Arendt has emphasized, power and violence are opposites: where the one rules absolutely, the other is absent. "Violence, being instrumental by nature, is rational to the extent that it is effective in reaching the end that must justify it. . . . It can serve to dramatize grievances and bring them to public attention. . . . Contrary to what its prophets try to tell us, violence is more the weapon of reform than of revolution."[17] However, violence can also be irrational, purely expressive rather than instrumental, a release of anger long repressed, a seizure of power long denied.[18] In any case, struggle, whether violent or not, will always be present as long as the human species continues to develop, and it will always be defended by one side and denounced as unjust and brutal by the other. Such struggle is rooted in the nature of our existence, since it is only by putting forth strength that we are both free and erring. The intransigent pacifist is thus in one sense a greater threat to peace than those who reckon with the existence of force and its inevitable exercise. To recognize this fact is not to give free reign to the brutality and moral irresponsibility of power. On the contrary, "if this situation is envisaged with the relentless realism of Christianity, which shies away from all utopianism, there is more hope that the immoral use of force can be less easily disguised under pretense of moral justification."[19] And this brings us now to ask what such Christian realism has to say about the perennial human dream of a better future.

III

I said at the beginning that the point of contact today between Christian faith and contemporary culture is our unfinished character as human beings, our peculiar capacity to create ourselves and our race anew. We can, if we so choose, make our future discontinuous with our present. Christianity has always recognized and approved this freedom in the case of religious conversion, but whenever it has been exercised in the social and political spheres, such freely chosen discontinuity has usually met with suspicion and rebuke. The historical reasons for this inconsistency are not hard to find. From an alienated minority Christians became, toward the end of the Roman Empire, the guiding elite of society. "Christendom" was in effect the union of church and society, resulting in the belief that submission to lawful authority was identical with submission to God. In this way the political order took on some of the immutable character thought to be possessed by the church herself. Coupled with this outlook was the static image of the world common for centuries, the conviction that the universe, as a work of God, could not be anything but ordered and complete. People were called upon not to transform but to inhabit it, not to build it but to adapt to it. It was God's initiative that counted in history, not man's. Looked at from this viewpoint the evils and inequalities of society due to human sinfulness were destined to endure; to oppose them was somehow to oppose what the divine will allowed. A certain passive element, which is indeed integral to Christian sensitivity to grace and its unpredictability, was thus gradually transferred to the political and social orders and came to mean that initiative could only be tolerated if it came from those already in possession of civil authority.

This explains why the view of man and his world as still unfinished was never an attractive concept to Christianity, especially Catholicism. Violence was often condoned by church officials against enemies of the *status quo*. Even today the Roman Catholic Church does not really recognize the essentially relative character of all institutional forms. (It is against this background, and as a reaction to it, that one has to judge the present tendency of some Catholics to support almost any attack at all upon the established order.) There is, moreover, the long tradition of Christian spirituality, from Augustine to Aquinas to John of the Cross, which spoke of holiness in terms of despising and rejecting the things of earth in order to draw nearer to God. This certainly explains why Christians have often tended to be people of yesterday, seeing only the dangers in change and giving the painful impression that they are "running mopishly and in a disgusted, critical mood behind the carriage in which the human race drives into a new future."[20] Only in this context can one understand how unusual is the growing realization today that personal religious conversion has to involve awareness of the social dimension of sin and redemption. Human structures, in other words, can objectify and even institutionalize that resistance to the Gospel message which each individual finds within him- or herself. Such a deprivatizing of the Christian message is suddenly becoming more and more widespread, based on the conviction that it is "no longer possible to look upon the private struggle for holiness and the social struggle for peace and justice as two struggles. They are inseparably two aspects of the one struggle for the victory of grace, inner and social, over concupiscence, inner and social."[21]

Theological efforts to grapple with this relationship of the Gospel to social conflict have stressed the need to scrutinize not Scripture and traditional teaching alone, as theology has usually done, but also the life, preaching, and historical commitment of the church. In this way theology would fulfill a prophetic function "in so far as it interprets historical events with the intention of revealing and proclaiming their profound meaning."[22] We would then have an understanding of faith derived from a critical reflection upon contemporary Christian existence. Orthopraxis (right action) would thus become as important for Christianity as orthodoxy (right thinking). "It is evident that thought is also necessary for action," says Edward Schillebeeckx. "But the church has for centuries devoted her attention to formulating truths and meanwhile did almost nothing to better the world. In other words the church focused on orthodoxy and left orthopraxis in the hands of nonmembers and nonbelievers."[23] If Christians show in their lives that their hope for the future is capable of making history conducive to salvation and not opposed to it, then these lives themselves will become an interpretation of Jesus' teaching just as authentic as the Scriptures and documents of the church. Such teaching will then be seen to have a very definite significance for the conflicting aspirations of men and society.[24]

Did Jesus himself ever deal with such conflicts in society? Although some scholars have maintained he was a Zealot, the great weight of historical evidence is against his having been a political revolutionary.[25] Nonviolence is woven into the whole fabric of the gospels: Jesus' purpose was clearly to convert men, not kill them. To think of him as a terrorist would be to contradict everything we know of his life and teaching. His death on the cross was the supreme example of overcoming violence by submitting to it. Nevertheless, to identify him with social and political conservatism is equally absurd. For Jesus advocated a profoundly radical change of values, not only in the personal transformation of individuals but also in Jewish society. This becomes clear from the fact that no distinction between politics and religion existed in Palestine at that time. Under attack was not only Roman authority, opposed by the violence of the Zealots, but also the corrupt temple priesthood, which had a religious and political stranglehold on the people and was opposed by the Pharisaic movement. This movement's success ultimately transformed the structure of Jewish society through the creation of the more democratic rabbinate and synagogue, and there is good reason to believe that Jesus participated in this general movement, in spite of his hostility to "the Pharisees" of the gospel accounts.[26] In any case, Jesus clearly challenged the priestly authority. The Temple in Jerusalem was a symbol of their oppressive system, and his assertion of his own authority in its courtyards was a direct rebuke, not to cultic impurity or sharp business practice, but to the political exploitation of God's people. The parable of the vineyard tenants, delivered during these same days, was obviously addressed to the priestly establishment and reads almost like a declaration of war.[27] Annas and Caiaphas certainly understood it as such, decided that Jesus was too dangerous a subversive, and had him executed.

What I have just said is not in the least meant to suggest that Jesus believed his Kingdom to be identified with the establishment of a new social order. His mission was much more radically the creation of a new man, the liberation of men and women through his death and resurrection from all those selfish hindrances to their freedom which we call sin. Yet this work of salvation inevitably had a social and political dimension, as had the life of Jesus himself. For there are not two histories for the human experience, one sacred and the other profane, but one single history, enveloped by the single creative and redemptive action of God. In so far as we are personally oppressed by sin, our culture too will be oppressed by misery, ignorance, injustice, and greed. As sinners we inevitably project malice into the world we create. Hence when the individual is freed from personal guilt, such liberation attacks at the same time the roots of sinful social situations, just as, conversely, a sinful milieu will tend to facilitate personal selfishness and pride. Jesus and his Kingdom therefore cannot be indifferent to whether a society is just or not.[28] Admittedly the perfect society, like the perfect man, is an eschatological event. Both must remain unfinished as long as time continues to change them. Yet secular men and women want to know what changes are to be made here and now; they refuse to accept either the individual or society as static. This forces the Christian to ask how such secular dreams can mediate between faith and social responsibility. In other words, how can both he and the secularist begin to dream the same dreams?

What we have here is obviously a task for the Christian imagination. Christians must connect their hopes of freedom from sin with hopes for the common destiny of mankind. Not that judgments in the social and political spheres are to be based upon concepts like salvation and the Kingdom of God; complex decisions in the public forum have to rely upon equally complex influences from national goals, economic policy, local interests, diplomatic pressures, and countless other factors. Nor will Christian hope allow any identification of Christ's Kingdom with the unavoidably ambiguous achievements of men. An ideology of political action does not cease to be finite and relative, and especially does not cease to be ideology, simply because those who believe in it add the adjective "Christian." Here precisely is the danger in using current liberation movements as a point of departure for theological reflection. Such phenomena may indeed reveal in a very striking way God's saving and liberating action, and to the extent they actually do, they become a "word of God" spoken to us here and now. Yet the phenomena themselves remain ambiguous, and it is extremely difficult for the theologian, in reflecting upon them, not to be influenced by ideological presuppositions. We may freely grant this danger and nevertheless insist that, constant though it is, it can never justify a failure of theological nerve. For the secular dream is in desperate need today of that eschatological sense of the new suddenly coming to birth. This specifically Christian contribution can rescue current secular imaging of the future from the Orwellian tendency to imprison human society in its own economics and science, as if these were some kind of physical laws to which it must inevitably submit, rather than objects of free political and social choice. To dream of a better future, let us repeat, simply has to involve more than the endless projection of present probability or the petty unfolding of a current technological trend.[29]

The Christian imagination is thus in a position to compensate for the current cultural loss of a sense of transcendence. Its strong eschatological bent introduces the concept of discontinuity into human affairs, enabling man in his thinking to breach the bonds of the predictable and to encompass the possibility of developments not dependent upon human resources alone. For while Christian faith and morality are operative only in and through the raw materials of public decision, they also involve a duty not encompassed by such decision, namely to find God whenever one finds one's neighbor. Conflict is to be found precisely because all human achievement is ambiguous. This is why the Christian ideal of peace and justice has nothing to do with merely tranquilizing the world. This ideal will always be one of striving, and it is by such striving that the religious person ultimately makes sense of his dreams as well as his faith. St. Paul expressed it well: "Hope would not be hope at all if its object were in view. How could a man hope for something which he sees? And if we are hoping for something still unseen, then we need endurance to wait for it."[30]

3

Play

In the last chapter I spoke of the inevitable conflict that arises when different men and women imagine, plan, and then seek to execute different futures for themselves and their world. Such conflict is the perennial experience of *homo faber,* the maker, the builder, the changer of institutions and culture. Since the Industrial Revolution and the rise of science and technology, this capacity to produce the useful and the new has developed beyond all expectation, and is apparently limited only by the amount of energy at our disposal. This is the realm of economics, government, and social reform, where the human race has its primary experience of freedom and where peoples will forever clash over the right to determine their destiny.

But there is another capacity in all of us besides this desire to make and to do, and it is precisely a desire to be free from such a desire, to escape the world of conflict and to experience that carefree harmony we once knew as children. This we try to recapture through leisure. Here we have the world not of inactivity but of activities for their own sake, the world of *homo ludens,* the player, who is free to be spontaneous and purposeless—no longer having to achieve but content simply to be. So evident are these two human capacities that it has become almost a cliché to point out the complementary nature of play and work, of harmony and conflict. Work and conflict produce the means of man's survival; play and harmony make that survival enjoyable and worthwhile. We have to alternate between these two worlds in order to be truly ourselves, since in each we actualize in a very different way our desire and longing to be free.

Yet if all this is readily acknowledged, if by nature we are fitted for both work and play, if both spring from our freedom and realize our potential, then why should we have such a problem today keeping the two in balance? American society, so obviously achievement-oriented, seems to be in especial trouble here. Why does the increase of leisure make us feel so ambivalent and uneasy? Why should the reward of so much effort result in boredom or guilt or both? The more the obligatory work week has been reduced, the longer hours executives seem to toil and the more laborers desire overtime. Financial necessity explains this in individual cases, but the phenomenon is so widespread that another necessity must be operative, a certain unfreedom regarding the use of time, a certain compulsion. The obverse of this can be seen when a person is unable to play, or plays compulsively, without real enjoyment or festivity. For to have free time clearly does not imply that it will be used freely. "Sunday neurosis" and "vacationitis" have become common terms for psychiatrists. "It is paradoxical," writes one, "that when man through scientific knowledge has become too efficient in securing with little effort the basic necessities of life, he becomes so deadly serious and looks nostalgically at the creative centuries of the past during which he still had the time and the detachment necessary for play and creativity. In this paradox lies the secret of understanding the crisis of Western civilization."[1]

One thing is certain for the future: there will be less energy to use and less work to do. With a four- and possibly even a three-day work week, overtime will disappear altogether and leisure will come into its own. There are signs that very few in the West are psychologically ready for this particular kind of "future shock." The role of play in human life has thus to be seriously reexamined. Let us see what we can learn about it from man's history, from his psychology, and from his Christian heritage.

I

Thoughtful persons have made what may strike us as some highly exaggerated statements about this role of play in human life. Here are some examples: "Man is a plaything in the hand of God," says Plato, "and truly this is the best thing about him. Everyone, therefore, whether man or woman, must strive towards this end and must make of the noblest games the real content of their lives. . . . What, then, is the right way of living? Life must be lived as play, playing certain games, making sacrifices, singing and dancing, and then a man will be able to propitiate the Gods, and defend himself against his enemies, and win in the contest."[2] Or consider this extraordinary text of another philosopher, Friedrich Schiller: "Man only plays when he is in the fullest sense of the word a human being, and he is only fully a human being when he plays."[3] The implication here is evidently that to speak of play is somehow also to speak of basic human nature. "For many years the conviction has grown upon me that civilization arises and unfolds in and as play," writes the historian Johan Huizinga in his classic study of the subject. "It is through this playing that society expresses its interpretation of life and the world. By this we do not mean that play turns into culture, rather that in its earliest phases culture has the play-character, that it proceeds in the shape and mood of play. In the twin union of play and culture, play is primary."[4] Very recently Josef Pieper began a volume on festivity with these words: "Certain things can be adequately discussed only if at the same time we speak of the whole of the world and of life. . . . Death and love are such subjects. Festivity too must be included in that category. This becomes apparent as soon as we try to get beyond mere description of facts."[5]

What are these facts? Let me enumerate at least four of them, and then perhaps the above statements will seem less exaggerated. The first, admitted by everyone, is that true play is an experience sought for its own sake, which contains its own inner meaning and is not thought of in terms of some purpose outside itself. This does not necessarily imply that such an experience can have no useful goals, since play obviously results in desirable things like relaxation and the renewal of energy for serious endeavor. The point is that these goals neither constitute nor exhaust the meaning of play, just as the biological usefulness of flowers and leaves as vital organs of plants is hardly an explanation for their extravagance in shape, color and smell, or for the extraordinary multiplicity of their species. Indeed, measured by the standard of utility, most of what we find in nature is only partially purposeful and much of it apparently purposeless. On the other hand, meaning is not at all to be measured either by usefulness or extraneous effects. For example, knowledge clearly has uses, but its meaning is rooted in itself: the possession of truth. Thus laws enacted by a government have an end in view, while jurisprudence does not; it seeks only truth in questions of law. Nor does art exist in order to provide a living for artists, though it does this too. Its meaning is simply that it should be, that it should faithfully reflect the beauty which the artist has caught. We see the same in the unselfconscious play of a child, "an unchecked revelation of its youthful life in thoughts and words and movements and actions. . . . That is what play means; it is life, pouring itself forth without an aim, seizing upon riches from its own abundant store, significant through the fact of its existence."[6]

These words well describe the carefree play of the child, but do they apply also to that of adults? Yes, because in the end the meaning of each is the same: an expression of personal freedom, not yet lost by the child but painfully limited in adult life by the pressures of social reality. Hence our second fact is that in play the adult tries to bridge the gap between the freedom he desires and the unfreedom he actually has. He is, as Erik Erikson says, a commodity-producing and commodity-exchanging being, whereas the child is only preparing to become one. The adult world is therefore one of pressure, tension, and continual concern with earning a living. A man or woman's role in society in fact tends to be defined by the work he or she does most of the time. Play is thus infrequent and constitutes that "narrow area within which our ego can feel superior to the confinement of space and time and to the definitiveness of social reality—free from the compulsions of conscience and from impulsions of irrationality. Only within these limitations can man feel at one with his ego."[7] For Erikson adult play is a re-creation, a periodic stepping sideways and away from those forms of defined limitation which are our social reality.[8] The result is bodily freedom, in so far as climbing or running give the sense of excess space; freedom from the pressure of time through lazy trifling or, in the case of competitive games, through time's regulation; freedom from the control of events through games whose rules we decide and which give to each player an equal chance to win; freedom, finally, from the conventions of everyday living, since free display of emotion is more easily indulged in as well as tolerated when the context is not the workaday world of the weighty and the earnest.

Nevertheless, while seriousness tends to exclude play, play itself can quite easily involve seriousness. This is the third fact to note, one which almost forty years ago was exhaustively documented by the masterful study of Johan Huizinga. The task he set himself was to analyze the play element in man's cultural history. What he found was that, insofar as play possesses the "agonistic" character of a serious contest, it permeates almost every aspect of civilized behavior and social structure. Such organized competition or *agon* formed the core of Hellenic social life, and like its counterpart of *paidia* (considered as pure play or aesthetic diversion) was largely devoid of purpose. What mattered in such contests was not the material result—the ball being in the hole—but the fact that the game had been successfully completed, that someone had actually won. Winning meant giving proof of superiority, showing oneself to be victor, thus gaining esteem and honor.

According to Huizinga the competitive instinct is not so much a will to dominate, which he says is always secondary, as it is a desire to excel.

This desire to excel may be seen most clearly today in competitive sports, but there also continues to be a "ludic factor" in education (the Latin *ludus* means both play and school), in the law courts (where justice is decided by contest), in music and the fine arts (when these become occasions to vie for prizes), and until very recently even in war (before "total war" disregarded the restrictive conventions of earlier times). The best workers in any field are still those who find their work to be a serious kind of "fun": the industrialist who "plays around" with economic possibilities, the financier who "plays the market," the philosopher who "plays" with ideas. And everyone recognizes that American and Russian efforts in space are at root a race for superiority, a kind of stylized play. "The nearer we come to our own times," concludes Huizinga, "the more difficult it is to assess objectively the value of our cultural impulses. More and more doubts arise as to whether our occupations are pursued in play or in earnest. . . . But we should remember that this precarious balance between seriousness and pretense is an unmistakable and integral part of culture as such. . . . There is nothing to prevent us from interpreting a cultural phenomenon that takes place with marked seriousness, therefore, as play." The reason for this ambiguity is that, "as a civilization grows more complex, more variegated and more overladen, and as the technique of production and social life itself become more finely organized, the old cultural soil is gradually smothered under a rank layer of ideas, systems of thought and knowledge, doctrines, rules and regulations, moralities and conventions which have lost all touch with play. Civilization, we then say, has grown more serious."[9]

This seriousness, however, in no way minimizes a fourth fact about play: it contains the risk and thrill of the unexpected. This adventurous character actually says much more about the player than it does about play itself. "Adventure is the result of the player's inner harmony," writes Robert Neale. "In the world of conflict there can be no delight in chance, risk, or striking events. . . . Spontaneity, surprise, and novelty upset the careful controls of the work self and produce the response of dread."[10] Thus while the play experience always involves antagonism of some sort, such conflict resides in the game, not in the player, or in the story, not in the characters (since play is often like the telling of a tale as opposed to the plotless life of work). Conflict within oneself, on the other hand, makes it far too painful to tolerate conflict outside, and therefore impossible to be playful toward life. Such a person usually has to win at all costs, and if he cannot, he will either cheat or quit. But an adventurer values the adventure itself and does not rely on any naïve promise of a successful outcome. He naturally seeks to win, but what interests him most is the thrill of the game. He is quite able to support the meaningful failure of a good plot which ends in the unexpected; what he cannot tolerate are failures that are random or routine. Huizinga points out that we are dealing here with an absolutely primary category of life: there is *fun* in such experiences of the unexpected.[11] "Fun" touches the very essence of play yet is a concept which resists all logical analysis. Pretending is simply pleasurable. There is deep human satisfaction in creating a world of illusion (the Latin *illudere* means "to be in play"), not by deceiving oneself but by thinking, feeling, and behaving in such a way that one designs and models an experience of the real very different from that which takes place in the world of work.

II

Up to now we have been dealing with some of the facts about play which one can learn from observation and reflection. The last fact, the element of adventure, underscores once more how much play is an attitude of mind as well as an objective event. Thus we focus again upon the vexing experience of larger and larger numbers today who see in occasions for play not a promise but a threat. "The trick is not to arrange a festival, but to find people who can *enjoy* it."[12] This aphorism of Friedrich Nietzsche highlights the problem more acutely: the typical modern seems to have much less talent for relaxation than for work; it is much more difficult for him to slacken effort than to increase it. A skill once possessed, the ability to be festive, has somehow been lost.

Not that we do not try. But our efforts to enjoy the luxury of being useless are frequently unsuccessful. In leisure a person may still feel as driven as he does in work. One has only to look at faces around the gambling tables of Las Vegas, or mingle with crowds along boardwalks on the New Jersey shore. They are all still at work. Free time does not really make them feel free but rather distracted and even compulsive. Vacationers at Catskill Mountain resorts or on American Express bus tours may not be there by force, but once there they are forcefully programed. "Play becomes a mode of doing nothing," writes one critic apropos of the dramas of Samuel Beckett, "a way of going on in the world in which all reasons for action have evaporated, in which the worth of action is itself questioned, in which there is nothing to be done." The three characters in Beckett's *Play* each tell a story filled with ulterior motives, deception, and betrayal. They speak from urns in center stage just as the characters of his earlier *Endgame* speak from trash cans. A fourth "character" turns out to be a single spotlight, and the three speak only in response to its focus. This "play" of the light is something the characters have to undergo, and without it there is no narrative. "The Other in Beckett's world is pictured as player, and Beckett's characters are the play of that Other. The Other, however, is experienced as absent. The play of the Other, then, is 'play without a player.' "[13]

Beckett's message of the absurdity of life gives us the obvious clue to our modern inability to be joyful and festive. "To have joy in anything," wrote Nietzsche shortly before his death, "one must approve everything." And conversely, "if it be granted that we say Yea to a single moment, then in so doing we have said Yea not only to ourselves, but to all existence."[14] Here we have the underlying reason for the human ability to celebrate some event, whether it be a birth, marriage, or homecoming, or discovering some person or place to be wonderful and warm. Life itself must be ultimately good. Otherwise, if we cannot approve the whole of it and buy it all, then neither can any single part be affirmed with serenity, much less rejoiced over with exuberance and love. "For all that has been—Thanks! To all that shall be—Yes!" These words from Dag Hammarskjöld's diary for 1953 are echoed by what he wrote there eight years later: "At some moment I did answer *Yes* to Someone—or Something—and from that hour I was certain that existence is meaningful and that, therefore, my life, in self-surrender, had a goal."[15] The person who faces his world unwillingly is by that very fact incapacitated for the intrinsically meaningful activity of play. When unable to work, such a one is desperate, because leisure becomes a burden too heavy to bear, something to be used up as quickly as possible by incessant entertainment or mindless distraction or the noisy pomp of the pseudofestival.

This need to approve the whole of life shows how far the spirit of play is from superficiality or mere frivolity. The latter Harvey Cox calls "the painted smile on a terminally sick patient. Its waggishness springs not from a joyous confidence in the ultimate goodness of life but from a despairing failure to make any sense out of it."[16] For often the goodness of living shines forth most brightly in the tragic, in the sudden shock of loss or death. The consolation which comes at such moments, usually from a religious conviction that all is nonetheless well with the world, is in a true sense a quiet form of rejoicing. But this happens only when grief and sorrow are accepted and affirmed as meaningful in spite of everything. The Black experience in America is a clear example of a whole people who were no strangers to oppression, yet who never lost the ability to celebrate with spontaneity and gratitude. Obviously culture, temperament, and religion are all contributing elements here, and we cannot expect to find the same outlook everywhere. Not every individual or people can experience with equal intensity what Miguel de Unamuno calls "the tragic sense of life." Where it is hardly present at all, however, where the excitement of triumph or the anguish of failure scarcely trouble the human heart, then capacity for festive exuberance will be correspondingly scant.

Hugo Rahner has written eloquently of this outlook, which he sees to be the true "psychography" of *homo ludens*. The source of a genuine ability to play, he says, is an "attitude that is poised between gaiety and gravity, between mirth and tragedy, and which the Greeks designated by the inimitable expression: *spoudogeloios*—the 'grave-merry' man. Such a man is capable of making his life into a game, and a very lovely one at that, because he knows that this life is either a comedy or a tragedy." The human being at play is thus able to blend jest with earnestness and to participate in the wisdom of ease and detachment, one "whose spirit is truly free . . . whose disappointments have turned into fun . . . with the easy step of one who has the earth at his feet and who no longer—by taking them too seriously—disfigures any of the values of this world."[17] Because play engages the whole of man, spirit as well as body, it becomes the perfect outward expression of this inward spiritual skill to be at the same time both serious and serene, to realize, however briefly, our deep-seated longing for psychic harmony.

Aristotle, and Thomas Aquinas after him, conceived this skill of the good player as nimbleness of mind and heart, and they both called it *eutrapelia*. Literally *eutrapelos* means "the well-turning man," someone Aristotle saw as "witty or versatile—that is to say, full of good turns; for such sallies seem to spring from the character, and we judge men's character, like their bodies, by their movements."[18] Eutrapelia is therefore a virtue which enables a person to play for the sake of seriousness. It represents a mean between the awkwardness of the boor and the clowning of the buffoon, between one who takes himself or herself too seriously and one who can take nothing seriously at all. This refined mentality is thus an elegance of movement, a kind of mobility of soul by which a cultured person "turns" to playful and relaxing things without losing himself in them. As such it is a sign of nobility of life and an essential attribute of the human ideal.[19]

This approach to play by thinkers like Rahner and Huizinga has been stoutly criticized as highly elitist and steeped in the comforts of high bourgeois culture.[20] Neither makes any secret of the fact that he deplores the utilitarian emphases in modern society, especially its regimentation and rigid technological structures. "Work and production became the ideal, and then the idol, of the age," writes Huizinga of the late nineteenth century. "All Europe donned the boiler-suit. Henceforth the dominants of civilization were to be social consciousness, educational aspirations, and scientific judgement."[21] There is obviously psychological blindness in such a comment, since it is surely possible to play in a boiler suit and—as I have already noted—to play with technology. But more importantly, there is social blindness: a divorce of the deep human experience of play from the toiling mass of humanity who have only since the last century begun to win their struggle upward. This experience cannot be seriously discussed today, much less enjoyed, aside from political and economic reality. "Are we not living in *one* world," asks Jürgen Moltmann? "Is it right to laugh, to play and to dance without at the same time crying out and working for those who perish on the shadowy side of life?"[22] Do not festivities and enjoyment freely indulged in by the affluent West appear in bad taste when contrasted with the indigence of the Third World? The point is well made, and highlights once more the clear interdependence of play experience and the human concern and serious effort to change our world for the better.

Interestingly enough, the novel which won Hermann Hesse the Nobel Prize, *Magister Ludi,* catches this ambiguity of play in a most striking way. Hesse tells the story of Joseph Knecht, the "game master," who lives in some future age and is a member of the aristocratic Castalian Order, the last stronghold of civilized men in a society perishing from a purely utilitarian view of life.

Members of the Order must learn to play the "Glass Bead Game" by which all knowledge is integrated and all spiritual values kept alive. Castalia is for Hesse the symbolic realm where culture thrives in splendid isolation, through pure play, untouched by the coarser realities of life. Yet these realities keep intruding. There comes to Castalia an emissary from the outside world, Plinio Designori, who argues with Knecht that a life consecrated exclusively to the mind is not only unfruitful but also dangerous. The scholar Fritz Tegularius, totally unfit for social responsibility, emerges as living example of an aestheticism cultivated without regard for the life of common people. Finally Knecht himself, near the end of his life, decides to leave Castalia, not because its spiritual ideal has proved false, but because he is at last aware of the social responsibility of the intellectual. Having attained the ideal by diligent efforts to "master the game," he now determines to put it back into the service of life and thereby set an example not only for the culturally poor but also for the culturally rich.

III

If we ask at this point what Christianity has to contribute to an understanding of the playful side of the human person, then we immediately come upon the close historical link between leisure and prayer. This is not to say that leisure and prayer were always associated with celebration and festivity. Christians have reacted no less ambiguously to the notion of play than have people generally. What was just said of eutrapelia, for example, certainly had no place in the ascetical tradition of the primitive church. A stern world renunciation was then the order of the day and continued as a dominant motif up to the Middle Ages, and even afterward remained dominant among Jansenists, Puritans, and the penitential monastic orders. "The pleasures of the table, of playing and joking, break down manly dignity," said Ambrose, Bishop of Milan. "Let us take care, when we are seeking mental relaxation, not to dissolve all the harmony of our good works." And John

Chrysostom was saying the same in Constantinople: "This world is not a theatre in which we can laugh; and we are not assembled together in order to burst into peals of laughter, but to weep for our sins. . . . It is not God who gives us the chance to play but the devil."[23] As we have seen, the medieval theology of the merry Christian developed fully only with Thomas Aquinas and his insistence that moderation in play was precisely Aristotle's virtue of eutrapelia, an ability to see the limits and inadequacy of all created things and so to be able to smile and laugh at them. Such a stance is not that of the worker but of the individual at rest. It is also the stance of the person aware of his dependence upon God, and such awareness is the starting point of prayer.

In this connection I am reminded of what W. H. Auden said about the spirit of carnival at a Columbia seminar in 1970. Carnival is the common celebration of our common fate as members of our species. Here we are, born into the world and destined to die, and this applies to everybody. Laughter is an act both of protest and of acceptance. There is indeed some joy in the fact that we are all in the same boat, with no exceptions made. Since our wish to have no problems is manifestly impossible, we laugh, and thereby simultaneously protest and accept. This laughter is especially appropriate before God, who is ultimately responsible for the comedy of life. The spirit of carnival, said Auden, is thus linked with the ability to pray. It is the total and festive acceptance of all that is ridiculous in the human experience. Who but God could have thought of all this? Yet in accepting the whole thing we do not understand it at all. A prayer of laughter is thus no more out of place than a prayer of complaint, because only God knows why he started it all or how it can possibly be an object of his love.

In the *Laws* Plato referred to man as the plaything of God, and the 7th century Greek abbot Maximus Confessor elaborated a whole mystical theology around this concept of the playing of God—a purely negative theology, it should be noted, ending up with imagery and symbols which acknowledge that we know we do not know. "Then was I beside him as his craftsman," says Proverbs of Divine Wisdom, "playing before him all the while, playing on the surface of his earth; and I found delight in the sons of men."[24] Yet this playing of God, incalculable and unpredictable, working in creative freedom untouched by necessity or constraint, has strange results. Things and people keep knocking into each other. This can annoy us and make us react angrily. But we can also see in this malfunctioning of life a comic aspect and accept it with good humor. Such surrender to the game of life clearly means surrender also to life's tragedy. "We ourselves," admits Maximus, "begotten and born like the other beasts, we who then become children and move forward from youth to the wrinkles of old age, we who are like flowers which last but for a moment and who then die and are transported into that other life—truly we deserve to be looked upon as a children's game played by God."[25]

The first thing which Christianity says about play, then, is that the nature of inward festivity is at bottom a religious problem: only one who feels secure in God can be truly light of heart. There can be no festivity if a man or woman does not believe in the essential goodness of things, for such ultimate goodness validates all particular goods. This is what impressed Boris Pasternak's Doctor Zhivago when he reflected upon the intoxication of life. "People worked and struggled, each set in motion by the mechanism of his own cares. But the mechanisms would not have worked properly had they not been regulated and governed by a higher sense of an ultimate freedom from care. This freedom came from the feeling that all human lives were interrelated, a certainty that they flowed into each other—a happy feeling that all events took place not only on earth, in which the dead are buried, but also in some other region which some called the Kingdom of God, others history, and still others by some other name."[26] At least for the Christian such an agreement with everything that is has always found its highest expression through ritual festivity, through the praise of God as creator of all. In Christian liturgy every prayer closes with the word *Amen*, the Yes of worshipers to life, and every *Alleluia* echoes their affirmation of being. "Jesus Christ," says St. Paul, "was not alternately 'yes' and 'no'; he was never anything but 'yes.' Whatever promises God has made have been fulfilled in him; therefore it is through him that we address our Amen to God when we worship together."[27]

For the Christian the Eucharist is thus the primary form of that security in God which is basic to adult play as well as adult prayer. This is why elements of play have always been present in the Christian ritual, such as sacred dance, the exuberance of song, and the complete absence of that restlessness which tends to accompany purposeful activity. Only our dour seriousness inhibits such elements, pulling us back to worship which is efficient, pragmatic, and dull. True liturgy, on the other hand, is a wasting of time for the sake of God. "To be at play, or to fashion a work of art in God's sight—not to create, but to exist—such is the essence of the liturgy."[28] In divine worship there is a sphere of superfluity which is the very opposite of utility. All is voluntary and unnecessary, without compulsion or calculation. This accounts for the phenomenon of rapture in such celebrations, even when not accompanied by intense emotion, the sense of being swept away outside of time, the same shattering of man's normal relationship to the workaday world as takes place through nonreligious festivity. It also accounts for the role of silence and rest during the Eucharist, the very opposite of that idleness and boredom which cause "restlessness" and the incapacity to play. "Leisure is a form of silence," writes Josef Pieper, "of that silence which is the prerequisite of the apprehension of reality: only the silent hear and those who do not remain silent do not hear. . . . For leisure is a receptive attitude of mind, a contemplative attitude, and it is not only the occasion but also the capacity for steeping oneself in the whole of creation."[29]

This mention of contemplation leads us to the second thing Christian tradition says about play, namely that, if it is truly a surcease from purposeful work, it will tend naturally to activate that intuitive sense in us which is so necessary for our psychic health as well as for prayer. Such "seeing" may not be thought of as playful, but all the elements of play are there. Whether it be the vision of an artist or the ecstasy of a saint or the wonder of someone lolling on the grass gazing at a bird or a sunset, such a moment is meaningful in itself, long before the unrest of thought tries to capture it in the clarity of a distinct idea. For these are all moments of complacency, of relaxing that strenuous gaze upon the particular required by the useful and the productive. Their inner meaning lies precisely in a deepened sense of mystery: the world is more profound and all-embracing than the logic of every-day reason had taught us to believe. Such moments activate that "strange power buried deep in man to carry on an inward dialogue between layers of his own being. It sorts over the raw experiences that come to him and . . . goads him to relate to his consciousness the mysterious wraith of mystery and wonder that hovers over them all."[30]

This capacity to scrutinize meaning, like festivity itself, enables one to escape the demands of an intrusive technological world and reach out for those life-renewing forces present in the whole of reality as well as in the human heart. When we reach out to God it becomes prayer. In both prayer and play earthly values are seen in their full transience and fragility, but whereas in meaningful play one becomes aware somehow of the limitless possibilities of life, in prayer one becomes aware of a Person. For the prayer's gaze is centered upon the divine. In the case of the Christian it is the person of Jesus who is "seen," for it is he who is, as Son, the pledge of that unimagined and incredible love of the Father which is the source of final rest. The joy of such knowledge is indeed wonder for the Christian, for wonder, as Aquinas points out, is precisely a longing for knowledge.[31] Contemplative prayer is thus an act of hope that we shall become what we "see" to be our destiny in Christ and that we shall grow in deeper understanding of both his person and his action in our lives.

This brings us now to a final contribution of Christian tradition to the understanding of play: its assertion that all the genuine human experiences we have been exploring in this chapter are in the end not of our own making at all, but are much more like gifts to be received with gratitude. The reasons are those I have touched upon already: the human condition is normally much more one of conflict than of harmony; we do useless and truly festive things only with difficulty; our adventures are few and far between; we play more through compulsion than through freedom, and our efforts to control our play inevitably result in more work. The true player is thus the man or woman willing to be surprised. Obviously we have to plan a vacation, organize a sporting event, prepare for a celebration, but when these events actually go as they should, when we actually experience delight and joy and peace and rest, and not merely pleasure, then we receive something that is not in human power to give. Josef Pieper has pointed out that this is the almost forgotten reason for the age-old custom of wishing one another well on great festival days. In wishing good health, happiness, and even a good appetite, the real thing we are wishing is the success of the celebration itself, not its outer forms and trimmings but the gift that is meant to be its true fruit: renewal, transformation, rebirth.[32] When this in fact takes place the only proper response is gratitude, which is itself a source of courage and hope for the person returning to the world of conflict and work.

This point of view is not at all easy for people who tend to overvalue hard work, or who can relax only with what they have acquired with trouble and toil. The effortless joy of true play seems an affront to their autonomy and self-sufficiency. For they want desperately to eliminate the element of surprise from their lives, to receive no gifts, to determine everything, to claim everything as their right. Christian tradition, on the other hand, sees the whole of life enveloped in the unpredictable workings of God's grace, and the surprise which comes from the joy of true play is simply the privileged awareness of a presence and an action which are there, unexperienced, all the time. This is why the

ancient writers spoke of the "game" of grace, the action of God
in Christ which is full of meaning and contentment, bound by no
necessity but only by love. "Unless you change and become like
little children, you will not enter the kingdom of God."[33] No one
is more eager to receive gifts than a child, and it is surely the child
in us who desires to play. Nor has the Christian ever ceased to
use the concept of play as the metaphor for the state of the blessed
in the world to come, where all is gift, rest, joy, and gratitude.
The words of Hugo Rahner sum this up well and will serve as our
conclusion: "In play," he says, "the mind is prepared to accept the
unimagined and incredible, to enter a world where different laws
apply, to be relieved of all the weights that bear it down, to be
free, kingly, unfettered and divine. Man at play is reaching out
. . . for that superlative ease, in which even the body, freed from
its earthly burden, moves to the effortless measures of a heavenly
dance."[34]

4

Failure

We have been discussing the experience of play as an escape from the world of achieving and an entry to the world of rest. Man the player regularly wants to be free of work, to be spontaneous and purposeless, not to make and to do but simply to be. Yet all the while we know that play is the exception and not the rule. Our work selves remain by far the larger part of our lives. Doing and achieving return as goals the instant festivity ends. These goals are in fact just as important as goals of harmony and peace, and whenever they elude us, we inevitably feel diminished and lost. None of us, in other words, can really be indifferent to success.

Our play consciousness is well aware that what we are doing may not turn out well; in every game or story there is always the risk and thrill of the unexpected. But our work consciousness is operative most of the time, and it does not make us feel adventurous at all: it is rarely willing to gamble and almost never willing to lose. Meshing these two selves is thus an impossible task. One cannot be both worker and player at the same time. The reason, as Robert Neale has argued, is that from a psychological point of view work is an attempt to resolve inner conflict, whereas play does not solve anything but is the *result* of such conflict resolution.

When we function well as workers, accomplishing the tasks we take on, then our psyche tends to slacken and rest, and we can move for a brief respite into the alternating rhythm of play.

But what if we fail? The significant thing is that we tend to think about failure in precisely this tentative way, as a question lurking in the back of our minds, a remote possibility whose actual arrival we greet with astonishment and dread. No one is more surprised at moral failure, for example, than the person who "works" at becoming morally better. Yet failure is just as endemic to life as achievement. As workers we do not make up the rules. And when we fail at something we cannot suddenly change them or walk away, as from a game which is over and done. The failure in question must be faced and lived with, whether it is physical, moral, psychological, or social. To deny or rationalize it away is to enter the world of make-believe. Nor are these blows to self-esteem and threats to future success to be attributed to some mysterious force outside ourselves called "fate" or "the breaks." Much less are they to be attributed to God, although from a Christian point of view, as we shall see, God is intensely interested in the loser, especially in what he or she does with the loss. No, we fail because *we* fail. "The fault, dear Brutus, is not in our stars but in ourselves."

The real difficulty is that we reflect so little upon this "fault." What should worry us is not its existence but our inability to understand and cope with it. How, we may well ask, does one become a good loser? Is there an art in losing well, in surviving blows to one's ego? Is one's religion to be used merely as a sedative to ease the pain? Or does being a Christian somehow make failure a qualitatively different human experience?

I

The judgment made at the grave of Willy Loman by his son at the end of Arthur Miller's *Death of a Salesman* summarizes a whole life lived within an unreal dream of overachievement: "He never knew who he was." Willy's tragedy is that he is driven by the American compulsion to win and will not allow either of his sons simply to be himself in the warmth and security of the unexceptional. A decade ago Daniel Boorstin wrote that we Americans use our wealth, our literacy, our technology, and our progress to create a thicket of unreality standing between us and the facts of life. The result is that losing of any type has almost become un-American. "Each of us individually provides the market and the demand for the illusions which flood our experience. We want to believe in these illusions because we suffer from extravagant expectations." We expect more than the world can give and therefore also too much of our power to shape it. The making of these illusions has actually developed into very respectable businesses: advertising, public relations, many of the activities which pretend to inform, comfort, improve, and educate. "Nowadays everybody tells us that what we need is more belief. . . . That may be true in the long run. What we need first and now is to disillusion ourselves. . . . We are haunted, not by reality, but by those images we have put in place of reality."[1]

Few forces in fact seem to dominate modern American life as does this fear of failure. A new periodical, *Prevention,* deals entirely with the most elaborate precautions to avoid even the threat of ill-health. In educational circles the I.Q. test is out and pass-fail is in (most often evolving into pass-incomplete). Educators are asked to eliminate, as much as possible, all real differences among students. Not until 1967 did the *Readers' Guide to Periodical Literature* list its first article under "failure." Before that year someone searching under this category would find "Failure—see Success." One of the reasons the Vietnam war proved so devastating for the national psyche was that we who had never lost a war were actually not able to win. We had always known, of course, that we would win in the end—for the "comeback" is also essential to the American dream, that turning of the tables on apparent failure. This desperate need to win and its good and bad effects on character form the theme of countless American novels from

An American Tragedy and *The Great Gatsby* to the more contemporary works of Saul Bellow and John Cheever. And where else but
in the United States would a major university organize a study to
dissect the anatomy of failure? In the fall of 1973 the Massachu-
setts Institute of Technology listed just such a course, called "Failure of Human Systems," launched by professor Frank P. David-
son. "I was struck," he said during a *New York Times* interview,
"that so many of the institutions of society are really set up to deal
with failure," and he cited courts, prisons, bankruptcy law, the
insurance industry, medicine, and the military.[2] His students explore the causes and effects of failure, examine its individual,
organizational, social, and ethical implications, and ponder ways
in which to cope with it. The implication is that the existence of
failure in the world is somehow the result of neglect. People have
not been *trying* to do away with failure so much as they have been
trying to do away with poverty, hunger, and overpopulation.
Surely (it is implied) more careful study by experts in all fields will
eventually unearth ways to prevent the failure of such systems, or
at least develop new methods to transform failing situations into
success.

Erik Erikson, to whose thought I have become increasingly
indebted in the course of this book, has traced this peculiarity of
the national psyche back to the extraordinary influence of the
frontier experience. Its seemingly limitless character caught the
popular imagination early. This must be seen, he says, as having
been combined with a certain religious puritanism, understood as
"a system of values designed to check men and women of erup-
tive vitality, of strong appetites, as well as of strong individuality."
The synthesis of these two disparate elements meant that American ego identity was finally based upon "some tentative combination of dynamic polarities such as migratory and sedentary, in-
dividualistic and standardized, competitive and cooperative,
pious and freethinking, responsible and cynical, etc." The average American thus tends to feel secure in his identity "as long as
he can present a certain element of deliberate tentativeness and

autonomous choice. The individual must be able to convince himself that the next step is up to him" and that he always has the choice of "turning in the opposite direction if he chooses to do so."[3] The result is an openness in the American character, which has to do with images of movement and space as well as of an ever expanding future. Our powerful technological culture reinforces all this and makes any image of containment and limitation extremely difficult to absorb. The restrictive puritanism just mentioned, however—a kind of Prometheanism in reverse, to use William Lynch's phrase—continues to be all-pervasive, fostering fear and even guilt for entertaining the desire to be Titans. Lynch himself is convinced that one of the major complications in the picture is precisely this rather extraordinary combination of the building and destroying strains in contemporary culture. There is a constant action and reaction of the Promethean impulse taking place as a drama in the psyche of everyone. "It is not melodramatic—because the picture is so clear—to say that it is a period of enormous energy and enormous contempt."[4]

Such self-contempt seems to be one of the bases of the most prevalent of all psychic maladies in this country today: depression. A recent survey by the National Institute of Mental Health revealed that as many as eight million people a year may suffer depression severe enough to merit being treated by a doctor, and over 250,000 Americans were hospitalized for the ailment in 1973.[5] Clinically depressed persons can feel guilt and hopelessness for periods of six months or more, and this in spite of the fact that they may be quite successful in their professional lives. The key symptom seems to be a negative *value* judgment on oneself following a correct negative judgment upon a given course of action or even upon one's character as a whole. Thus, "I made a mistake" becomes "I never do anything right," and "I am a weak person" becomes "It's disgusting to be weak." This attaching of a negative value to one's deficiency promotes self-distrust, lowered self-esteem, and convictions of personal inadequacy. Routine human failure in things like examinations, love affairs, or jobs makes depressed people react as if their inmost egos had been fatally battered. Much more serious is that sense of failure which is not routine: the successful businessman who suddenly realizes that everything he has worked for in life is too fragile and inadequate to satisfy him and that life itself has become totally empty. In his case it may indeed be too late to learn that deficiency is simply human, and that everyone must eventually submit to what Ursula Niebuhr has called "the discipline of non-fulfill- ment."

I have been making the point that failure of all kinds is a normal human experience which Americans seem to have special diffi- culty in integrating into their lives. They believe more easily than others that nothing must get in their way, and when something does, they are more likely to be angry, guilt-ridden, or depressed. Jung has described this outlook as clinging to childhood levels of consciousness and resisting that extension of life's horizon which is the essential feature of maturity. Expectations of the immature are usually exaggerated, difficulties underestimated, optimism un- justified. "Whoever protects himself from what is new and strange and thereby regresses into the past, falls into the same neurotic condition as the man who identifies himself with the new and runs away from the past. . . . In principle both are doing the same thing; they are salvaging a narrow state of consciousness. The alternative is to shatter it with the tension inherent in the play of opposites . . . and thereby to build up a state of wider and higher consciousness."[6] To avoid this shattering, however, we tend to limit ourselves to the attainable, renouncing all other potentialities and thus losing valuable pieces of our past or future. In fact, says Jung, whenever it appears that the serious problems of life are being solved, we have a sign that such loss has already occurred. For these problems are not really meant for solution but for incessant attention and concern. Constant working at them is the only way we can be saved from stultification and petrifaction. Hence "my aim is to bring about a psychic state in which my patient begins to experiment with his own nature—a state of fluidity, change and growth, in which there is no longer anything eternally fixed and hopelessly petrified."[7]

To "limit oneself to the attainable" is, of course, to avoid failure. But it is also to avoid freedom. Whenever there is flight from this burden there is always a price to be paid. For such recoiling before the unknown, before the threat of sacrifices and loss, is to leave the beaker of life half empty, too many of its experiences unsavored, and above all to overlook that essential fact which Jung underscores, that the achievements which society rewards are won at the cost of a diminution of personality. William Lynch makes the same point when he says that there is a tyranny of past events which shapes and traps our images of the present. This ubiquity of dead images has to lie exposed before we can transform their old rigidities into new hypotheses. Freedom to cope with oncoming reality can only result from the ability constantly to change these images. There is much wisdom, therefore, in the following recollection from the early life of a very keen observer of the human psyche.

> Years ago I used to notice the differences among motormen on the Indiana Avenue streetcar line in Chicago—a street often blocked by badly parked cars and large trailer trucks backing into warehouses and maneuvering in everybody's way. Some motormen seemed to expect to be able to drive down Indiana Avenue without interruption. Every time they got blocked, they would get steamed up with rage, clang their bells and lean out of their cars to shout at the truck drivers. At the end of the day these motormen must have been nervous wrecks; I can imagine them coming home at the end of the day, jittery and hypersensitive, a menace to their wives and children. Other motormen, however, seemed to expect Indiana Avenue to be heavily blocked—a realistic expectation, because it usually was. They would sit and wait for minutes without impatience, calmly whistling a tune, cleaning their fingernails, or writing their reports. In other words, confronting the same objective situation, some motormen lived a hellish life of anger and nervous tension; other motormen had a nice, relaxing job, with plenty of time to rest.[8]

II

Thus far I have underscored the inevitability of failure in any full life but have not yet dealt with its roots or with the impact of its blows to our ego. As we shall see, the problem is how to follow the advice of Sirach: "My son, with humility have self-esteem; prize yourself as you deserve. Who will acquit him who condemns himself? Who will honor him who discredits himself?"[9] To survive the humiliation of failure we have to see it as an exposure of a fallibility so innate to human life that whenever it is fled from or denied we contradict part of ourselves. To describe this existential condition Paul Ricoeur uses geological images: there is in the essence of human nature a gap, a break, a breach, a rift, which is ultimately responsible for its errancy and wandering, its going astray, its becoming divided against itself. Other observers like Erich Fromm and Reinhold Niebuhr speak of our disequilibrium, the dichotomy between two orientations of the spirit, downward toward finitude and rootedness in nature and upward toward transcendence. Invariably, though unnecessarily, we seek security by overemphasizing one or other side of this polarity, and the ambiguity of this double movement is what leads us to "fail," whether physically, morally, socially, or psychologically. It will be worth our while to follow out some of the implications of this primordial disproportion.

On the side of our finitude, says Ricoeur, we have the notion of character, which is the narrowness of my individual experiential capacity in contrast to the openness of my humanity. This openness is my fundamental accessibility to all values of all men in all cultures, the whole range of the human, in other words a total transcendence of finitude. "I am capable of every virtue and every vice; no sign of man is radically incomprehensible, no language radically untranslatable, no work of art to which my taste cannot spread." My humanity is thus my community with all that is human outside myself. Nor is my character the opposite of that humanity, but rather that humanity "seen from somewhere,

the whole city seen from a certain angle, the partial totality."
While all values are in principle accessible to all men, I reach out
for them in a way necessarily peculiar to me. This is the sense in
which we can say that "each" man is "man." It follows that the
individuality of my character cannot be understood apart from its
universal humanity any more than I can separate the narrowness
of a particular point of view from its openness to a larger
panorama or to a horizon of endless perceptibility. This horizon,
as seen from any given individual's point of view, Ricoeur calls
happiness. Because this is what is looked upon rather than the
narrowness of my vision—the latter being an origin, not an object
—my immediate consciousness is not of limitation but of movement away from it, and it is this movement that tends to "hollow
an infinite depth in my desire." Thus the idea of totality begins
to dwell in the human will and to become the source of the most
extreme disproportion, preying upon human action and stretch-
ing man out between the finitude of character and the infinitude
of happiness.[10]

It is precisely failure that forces us back upon this finitude and
brings us to an acute awareness of our limitation. This can be seen
most clearly in the radical fragility of the triple quest that makes
us human: for possessions, power, and worth. All three are experienced as conflict and restlessness in the human heart. When
shall I have enough possessions? How much power do I want?
When will I be sufficiently appreciated and recognized? The object of any one of these quests can suddenly become the "all" of
unlimited desire. Consider, for example, how vanity perverts the
normal human quest for esteem. In itself the quest is a simple
desire to exist through the favor of another's recognition. The
fragility of such existence, however, is that what establishes it is
merely opinion. For nothing is easier to wound than an existence
at the mercy of a belief. Precisely because it is believed, one's
worth may be feigned or alleged, neglected or disputed, scorned
or humiliated. Yet we instinctively search for our own self-esteem
in and through this valorizing regard of others: I believe I am

worth something when the eyes of another approve my existence. How easy it thus becomes for an opinion as fragile as this to be driven by a passionate striving for honor, and for the vital affirmation of self to have grafted onto it the vainglorious quest for adulation. "One might say that the infinitude of happiness descends into the indefiniteness of restlessness. . . . Here is the source and occasion of every mistake and all illusion. . . . Only a being who wants the all and who schematizes it in the objects of human desire is able to make a mistake, that is, take his object for the absolute."[11]

Human fallibility, then, is rooted in that restive quality of the psyche always in movement toward an ideal which is logical and thinkable but not possible. Theoretically we seem destined for a full development of personality and talent. But for this actually to happen there would have to be a miraculous combination of circumstances: the world and everything in it would have to be perfect. Short of this there is no avoiding those traumatic elements that condition the psychology of children, or those errors of judgment which bring to naught the plans of adults, or that moral fragility by which we willfully do evil to our fellow men. At every level the human is radically unfulfilled and incomplete, a situation one author has called the "ontological definition of evil."[12] "Oh, the continent of a man," cries William Golding through his protagonist in *Free Fall*, "the peninsulas, capes, deep bays, jungles and grasslands, the deserts, the lakes, the mountains and the high hills!" Alienation of every type permeates our culture, persuading us that we are alone, lost, and unconnected. This has almost become a central feature of human existence, set in bold relief by the brutal power of psychology to clarify but not to explain. Self-awareness, reason, and imagination have thus "made man into an anomaly, into the freak of the universe. He is part of nature, subject to her physical laws and unable to change them, yet he transcends the rest of nature. He is set apart while being a part. . . . Reason, man's blessing, is also his curse; it forces him to cope everlastingly with the task of solving an insoluble dichotomy. Human existence is different in this respect from all other organisms; it is in a state of constant and unavoidable disequilibrium."[13]

This complexity and mystery of the human condition is ultimately the reason that a kind of hopelessness inevitably invades certain segments of life. The plain fact for all of us, as William Lynch has pointed out, is that many things are without hope, many people we are inclined to depend on cannot give hope, and many isolated moments do not themselves contain hope. There are times when the only genuine stance is one of total passivity before a destructive experience, and this is not opposed but correlative to the more normal stance of initiative. Human development is not possible, it seems, unless the individual passes through situations of humiliation and diminishment, of mistrust, doubt, and confusion. Maturity in these instances does not come so much from victory, says Erikson, as from synthesis. These negatives are not to be vanquished but integrated into a delicate balance with one's strengths. This is done through actually "living a *Passion:* that total passivity in which man regains, through considered self-sacrifice and self-transcendence, his active position in the face of nothingness, and thus is saved. Could this be one of the psychological riddles in the wisdom of the 'foolishness of the cross'?"[14] Erikson's role for the ego is precisely to seek this sense of wholeness through an active mastery over vicissitudes from without and impulses from within. "In his dreams, his play, his poetry and his rituals man is always trying to weave together . . . a meaningful and manageable whole out of the frightening welter of life's experiences."[15]

The lows of life, then, must be held on to with the same tenacity as the highs, not as if both can be kept together at rest but rather by accepting the constant dialectical tension between them. Otherwise the highs will never have modesty or reserve, and the way will be paved for those inevitable blows to excessive self-esteem. True identity can therefore never be found if anything in one's past is repudiated or forgotten. In fact, the more finite these past lows, the more our rootedness is manifested, our uniqueness strengthened, and our future possibilities affirmed. This is Erikson's formula for basic trust in the world: an openness and receptivity grounded on belief that life's failures and frustrations will not in the end outweigh its satisfactions. All of man's initiative and energy must be grounded on such prior passivity, for in this way he learns to endure limitations to his autonomy without losing, through excessive shame or self-doubt, basic confidence in his power to exercise it.[16] Ultimately this hope finds its highest articulation in a religious image based on belief in God. And it is to such belief that we shall now turn. For if I experience this hope as a Christian, then I have, along with urgent counsels to perfection, examples of the most compassionate attitude toward weakness of every kind and the very strongest assurance of divine support in the pain, failure, and frustration of life.

III

Dorothy L. Sayers is perhaps best known as a master of the detective story and creator of that most urbane of sleuths, Lord Peter Wimsey. By the mid 1940's she had made enough money at such writing to return again to what she had trained for in her student days at Oxford—a textual study of Dante. A decade later she had completed a new translation of *The Divine Comedy* and thereafter wrote several volumes of religious essays and plays. She was once asked what the study of Dante had taught her about life. She replied that she had learned the meaning of the birth and death of Jesus. God, she said, "had the honesty and courage to take his own medicine. Whatever game he is playing with his creation, he has kept his own rules and played fair. He has himself gone through the whole of human experience. He was born in poverty and died in disgrace, and thought it well worthwhile."

We have been discussing up to now the inevitable insufficiency rooted at all levels of the human makeup, as this has been spelled out for us by modern philosophy and psychology. Christianity is keenly aware of this fallibility and speaks to it by announcing that Someone Else has entered this search of ours for a seemingly hopeless fulfillment. Christians have never denied the radical inquietude of the human creature or the intolerable tension which is sometimes the result. What they do deny is that there is any mortal solution to this problem: it is not meant to be solved by human effort but only by the freely given, gracious intervention of God. The profoundly mysterious character of the dilemma is thus revealed, as well as the strange logic of Christian hope. Faced with an abundance of senselessness, failure, and frustration, the Christian insists upon a superabundance of meaning, an excess of sense over nonsense, even in the most desperate situations. Ultimately such logic is based upon the eschatological event of the risen Christ and the anticipation through history of the resurrection of all from the dead. More immediately, however, it is based upon the tenacious will to happiness that demands and expects fulfillment beyond anything reasonably attainable. St. Paul's rhetorical device of the Adam-Christ parallel in *Romans* speaks directly to this brokenness at the heart of human action: "If because of one man's fault, death reigned through that one man, how much more will those who receive the abundance of grace, the free gift of righteousness, reign in life through the one man Jesus Christ. . . . Law came in to increase the fault; but where sin increased grace abounded all the more."[17]

The irrationality in Christian hope is therefore its persistence in spite of all evidence to the contrary, preferring "passion for the possible" to brooding over the irrevocable. This formula of Kierkegaard stands in stark contrast to any wisdom of the present and illumines the central importance of promise to the experience of freedom. The ethical consciousness does not know of this hope for the radically new, says Paul Ricoeur, but the religious consciousness does, entrusted as it is to the "God who comes." "This logic of surplus and excess," he insists, "is to be uncovered in daily life, in work and in leisure, in politics and in universal history. The 'in spite of' which keeps us in readiness for the denial is only the inverse, the shadow side, of this joyous 'how much more' by which freedom feels itself, knows itself and wills itself to belong to the economy of superabundance."[18] Hence for the man of faith failure of every kind becomes part of a divine pedagogy for the human race, something not to be eliminated so much as incorporated into the promise of universal resurrection from the dead. The "game" God is playing with us is not one to be coped with intellectually. Our disillusionment with life is not meant to be calmed but overwhelmed. This outpouring of love which makes everything new was well known to Isaiah: "See, I am doing something new! Now it springs forth, do you not perceive it? In the desert I make a way, in the wasteland, rivers."[19]

This is the context in which Christianity has always placed the experience of moral failure and its subsequent sense of guilt. Man's sinfulness is the occasion for the most extraordinary outpouring of God's wisdom and mercy. "God has imprisoned all in disobedience that he might have mercy on all," says St. Paul. And he adds immediately, "How deep are the riches and the wisdom and the knowledge of God! How inscrutable his judgments, how unsearchable his ways!"[20] This was what Thomas Aquinas had in mind when he said that the fundamental malice of sin is the desire not so much to be equal to God as to be under no obligation to him, to escape from his bounty, to rely on one's own powers and to seek one's happiness by oneself.[21] This is why contemporary culture, to the degree that it draws support from the Promethean pretension to be master of one's life, inevitably tends to deny man's sinfulness. Christianity, on the other hand, far from eliminating the consciousness of sin, seeks rather to deepen it, precisely in order to illumine the love and mercy of God. The sacrament of "penance" has always been much more a sacrament of forgiveness.

It is therefore pure caricature to think of Christian reconciliation as a kind of vacuum cleaner removing superficial grime, so that we find ourselves in the end blameless after all. Our sins are not a kind of operational accident in which we are not really implicated, but manifestations of a sinful condition which is ours by reason of being human. Nor is Christian peace a kind of catharsis that comes from "getting everything off one's chest." It is rather a humble confession that I am *simul justus et peccator,* justified while remaining sinful, and that my trust is in the power and grace that come from the passion of Christ. "Man's knowledge of God without an awareness of his own wretchedness leads to pride," says Pascal. "An awareness of his wretchedness without the knowledge of God leads to despair. The knowledge of Jesus Christ represents the middle state, because we find in it both God and our wretchedness."[22]

To affirm one's freedom, then, is to take upon oneself the origin of evil. And this serves only to deepen the mystery all the more. "I cannot even understand my own actions," exclaims St. Paul. "I do not do what I want to do but what I hate."[23] Much of the appeal and fascination of William Friedkin's film of *The Exorcist* is due to the fact that, while it shockingly acknowledges the presence of evil in the world, it also locates it in a particular place, in the body of an innocent young girl. The story thus nourishes the conviction that ultimately it is not we who are responsible for the evil we experience, but that this is rather outside ourselves, in a wicked being who can somehow be controlled by magic. Whereas, on the contrary, there exists only the evil done by me, and its acknowledgment lays bare all the weakness, vulnerability, and inadequacy of my human psyche, an inexorable blending of wheat and cockle which are both to grow together until the final harvest. In vain do we try to express in facts and figures such inner disorder. This is why our confessions are necessarily very imperfect signs of what God actually forgives. For what we are dealing with here is not individual sins so much as a sinful state, an ever present and permanent reality referred to in the biblical texts on "original" sin. This "sin of the world," to use the Johannine phrase, stands as that mysterious dark side and counterpart of the luminous mystery of redemption in Christ.[24] "If we say, 'We are free of the guilt of sin,' we deceive

ourselves; the truth is not to be found in us. But if we acknowledge our sins, he who is just can be trusted to forgive our sins and
cleanse us from every wrong."[25] This is why "for our sakes God
made him who did not know sin, to be sin, so that in him we might
become the very holiness of God."[26]

It is not only this objective sinfulness that must be placed in the
context of God's mercy, but also the more subjective experience
of guilt. While the former is almost an ontological dimension of
existence, a collective reality in which the whole community is
implicated, the latter is much more individualized, a sense of
moral failure which is intensely personal. As such, says Paul Ricoeur, it is a graduated consciousness: we are wholly and radically
sinful, but more or less guilty. This is why feelings of guilt are
sometimes misleading, telling us more about our ideals than
about our actual moral condition. To recognize that we have
fallen short of these ideals is in itself a healthy disposition involving responsibility for the failure, repentance, and the seeking of
pardon before God. The problem, however, is that such a seemingly simple process can become enormously complex and difficult because of the terrible blow to self-esteem involved in the
admission of guilt. "The more real the guilt, and the closer to the
wellsprings of personality, the more it is dissimulated."[27] Here
we have the root of neurosis, that compulsive effort to disown past
wrongdoing by denying it, hiding it, ignoring it, or explaining it
away, all under the morbid illusion of impeccability. Could anything be more hopeless? The churches are not without blame
here, for often such neurosis is church-bred, brought on by the
rigidity and legalism of moral doctrine and the morose preaching
about damnation which usually goes along with it. The fifth peti-
tion of the Our Father, on the contrary, takes for granted both sin
and pardon, but then obliges us to extend to those who injure us
the same compassion and love which we have received from the
Father. Repentance, in other words, must finally be seen as something directed not only toward God but also outward toward
others. Situated in this way, guilt is caught up in a movement of

promise for the future and bears no resemblance at all to that remorse which gnaws from within and broods over failures of the past.[28]

The Christian thus situates human deficiency and failure within the loving presence of God. He can affirm with Jeremiah, "More tortuous than all else is the human heart, beyond remedy; who can understand it?" Yet he listens also to the consolation of Isaiah: "I am the Lord, your God, who grasp your right hand; it is I who say to you, 'Fear not, I will help you.' Fear not, O worm Jacob, O maggot Israel; I will help you, says the Lord."[29] The Christian does not imagine that there can be heights in man without corresponding depths, much like the breaches and rifts of which Ricoeur speaks. He knows that in human life shadows belong to the light and evil belongs to the good. Above all his faith tells him that evil is part of the economy of superabundance and that he must have the courage to incorporate his failures, moral and otherwise, into a promise of hope. Unlike the strict moralist, the Christian views the evils of life as part of God's providence, confident that the fate we do not welcome can become the ground for future creativity, and that all events work mysteriously toward the advancement of God's Kingdom. This is why Augustine's *Confessions* can be both an avowal of sin and guilt as well as testimony to the mercy of God and praise for the divine wisdom. For him who believes, "history is the business of making personalities, even so to speak by putting them through the mill; . . . its very vicissitudes bring personality itself to a finer texture."[30]

What, then, have we learned about failure? Actually not much we did not already know. It is part of every man and woman's life; it is frequently a better teacher than success; if there is an art in losing, it probably lies somewhere between making an absolute of success and a cult of failure. Yet this common lot of mankind, which occurs almost daily in some form, is what provided the great theme of Greek tragedy: the inevitability of defeat and the triumph of surviving it. This can be in as low a key as the quiet

remark of Adlai Stevenson after losing the presidential election
of 1952: "I felt like a little boy who had stubbed his toe in the
dark. He was too old to cry, but it hurt too much to laugh." Or
it can be as sublime as the passion of Jesus, whose acceptance of
defeat was the occasion for an outpouring of God's love and a
manifestation of his power to triumph over the ultimate failure of
death. For as William Lynch has said, limitations are the path to
whatever the self is seeking, to insight, to beauty, to fulfillment.
It is a path both narrow and direct, leading as it must through
acceptance of all that is finite, our projects that go awry, the
friends who give no support, all our own physical, mental, and
moral fragility. Here is the central puzzle of man, a puzzle to be
worked at indeed, but to which in the end God alone has the key.
The Psalmist says it well: "As a father has compassion on his sons,
the Lord has pity on those who fear him; for he knows of what
we are made, he remembers that we are dust."[31]

5

Old Age

The fallibility we have just discussed is exemplified in a most extraordinary way by the experience of growing old. Yet it is no secret that old age, as we are coming to know it today, is a largely uninvestigated period of human life. The reason is not that old people have not in the past been the occasions for much social, medical, and familial concern, but rather that their problems have been seen almost exclusively as social, medical, and familial. In recent years, however, their very numbers have begun to force upon us a new perspective. In the United States alone there are now twenty million over 65, almost a third of these over 75, and by 1980 there will be five million more—over 10 percent of the population as opposed to 4 percent in 1900. Practically no one "retired" in 1900, since the average man or woman was dead at 40. Now everyone plans retirement, since the average life span is 70. This means that the whole structure of society is changing. More importantly it means that larger and larger numbers of men and women have to face a time of life experienced formerly by relatively few. A human life lived until 70 or 80 is qualitatively different from one lived until 40 or 50; old people are qualitatively different as men and women from their younger selves. Yet how little is really known about what it means to be human in old age! It is "the last great unexplored frontier in human experience."[1]

In her remarkable study of aging, Simone de Beauvoir says that "the whole meaning of life is in question in the future that is waiting for us: if we do not know what we are going to be, then we cannot know what we are."[2] In the following pages I shall not speak about society's treatment of old people, important as this topic obviously is, but rather about what the experience of old age has to tell us about our own lives, regardless of age. Let us begin with elements of the human problem as these have come into sharper focus in recent years and then focus on some of the resources, both psychological and spiritual, which are at hand to deal with it. We will then be in a better position to understand the significance of passivity for human life, as well as the importance of old age for man's relationship with God.

From the very start there must inevitably be a touch of sadness in our discussion, not unlike the sadness of bereavement. For old age too involves loss, and what is lost here is part of ourselves. Along with the joy that comes with living many years there is also grief. To anticipate this can almost be as painful as trying to accept it. The poet Gerard Manley Hopkins caught this feeling in the following lines written to a young child who mourned the falling of autumn leaves:

> Margaret, are you grieving
> Over Goldengrove unleaving?
> Leaves, like the things of man, you
> With your fresh thoughts care for, can you?
> Ah! as the heart grows older
> It will come to such sights colder
> By and by, nor spare a sigh
> Though worlds of wanwood leafmeal lie;
> And yet you will weep and know why.
> Now no matter, child, the name:
> Sorrow's springs are the same.

Nor mouth had, no nor mind, expressed
What heart heard of, ghost guessed:
It is the blight man was born for,
It is Margaret you mourn for.[3]

I

The philosopher Douglas Steere, himself well into his seventies, underlined the human problem we are dealing with when he said to me once, "Old age is not for sissies." Growing old is indeed quite as difficult a task as growing up, and as much of a challenge to the human person as adolescence, young adulthood, or middle age. Yet often it is not seen as such. What usually occurs, as men and women advance in years, is a denial of the aging process, a refusal to admit either that one is getting old at all or that old age is a distinctive period of life into which one is eventually forced by time. This refusal continues until some physical or social disability imposes recognition, if not dejected resignation. According to Erik Erikson even Western psychology has until recently avoided looking at the range of man's whole life cycle, mainly because the West, unlike the East, really does not cherish any concept of the whole life.[4] The values of American culture add to the problem, for Americans evade old age and conceal it almost in the same way they do death; both have become shameful secrets unseemly to mention. The enforced leisure of the old can never be seen as the task it is if a man or woman's real worth is measured exclusively by their productivity. Meaning or lack of it for old age therefore puts both individual and society to the test, as Simone de Beauvoir has noted. For this is what reveals meaning or lack of it in the entirety of life leading up to that old age, and uncovers the naked and often carefully hidden truth about a society's real principles and aims. Knowingly or not, she adds, we prepare a given old age for ourselves right from the beginning. Chance may change this, but in so far as it depends on us, we have already defined our final years by our way of life.[5]

Old age, then, is the prolongation and last stage of a certain process. Is this ending a waiting for death or a continuity of life, the termination of growth or a new opportunity for growth, like adolescence and middle age? Everything will depend upon whether "growth" is understood in terms of the person or in terms of the acquisition of status and material possessions. For by and large old people no longer *do* anything, they just *are.* How they think, or have always thought, of their growth and development is therefore of the utmost importance. Simply finding or creating things to be done as "therapy" for enforced idleness, valuable as this is in many cases, will not ultimately be of much help unless such things are seen as relating a man or woman to some larger human purpose and not relegating them to the status of second-class persons living on the periphery of life. Otherwise massive resentment can develop against the young and healthy, the "achievers," coupled with continual criticism of their projects and conduct. The bitterness of so many old people, their cynicism, obstinacy, and self-righteousness, is frequently a mask for their own self-hatred and despair of finding any reason for continuing the effort of life.

What meaning then is to be found in old age? In what direction is growth and fulfillment still possible so late in life? The self-hatred and despair of the overaged to which I have just alluded is attributed by Erikson to the lack or loss of what he calls accrued ego integration. The achievement of such "integrity" is precisely the task that is set by life before all who reach maturity of years. This task he describes as

> the acceptance of one's one and only life cycle as something that had to be and that, by necessity, permitted of no substitutions. It thus means a new, a different love of one's parents, free of the wish that they should have been different, and an acceptance of the fact that one's life is one's own responsibility. . . . Although aware of the relativity of all the various life styles which have given meaning to human striving, the possessor of integrity is ready to defend the dignity of his own life style against all physical and economic

threats. For he knows that an individual life is the accidental coincidence of but one life cycle with but one segment of history; and that for him all human integrity stands or falls with the one style of integrity of which he partakes.[6]

From a religious point of view, of course, such a coincidence of a given life with a given culture is not "accidental" at all, but I shall deal with this added perspective further on. Just now it is important to note that for Erikson the despair of old age, especially the fear of death, is to be traced directly to the fact that a person's one and only life cycle is not accepted as the ultimate of life. "Despair expresses the feeling that the time is short, too short for the attempt to start another life and to try out alternate roads to integrity. Such a despair is often hidden behind a show of disgust, a misanthropy, or a chronic contemptuous displeasure with particular institutions and particular people—a disgust and a displeasure which . . . only signify the individual's contempt of himself."[7] The "sense" of life a person has had before he grows old may thus have to be drastically redefined if he finds he is unable to accept the totality of his life as the only one he will ever have. Frantic efforts to develop an identity other than the one he has lived with for years will therefore involve painful conscious experiences, odd behavior patterns, and unconscious inner states which are disruptive of his emotions and person. Erikson would say that such a person's life to some degree lacked "basic trust," by which he means a simple sense of one's own trustworthiness and a reasonable trustfulness as far as others are concerned.[8]

Erikson's name for the true "sense of life" in old age is wisdom, "a detached concern with life itself in the face of death itself." This involves the ability to maintain and convey the integrity of experience in spite of the decline of bodily and mental functions, the ability to envisage human problems in their entirety: the "phrenosis" of Aristotle, wisdom which cannot be transmitted because not abstract. Above all such wisdom enables the old man or woman to represent to the coming generation a living example of the "closure" of a style of life. "Only such integrity can balance the despair of the knowledge that a limited life is coming to a conscious conclusion, only such wholeness can transcend the petty disgust of feeling finished and passed by, and the despair of facing the period of relative helplessness which marks the end as it marked the beginning."[9] Not that each and every old person must achieve such wisdom in its fullness, but there must be *some* wisdom, *some* integrity for life to close well. While the particular *style* of integrity will obviously be suggested by one's historical and cultural place, Erikson believes nonetheless that a wise Indian, a true gentleman of wealth, and a mature peasant would share and recognize in one another this final stage of integrity. The meaning of old age is thus to be found in this knowledge of how to close life well, and such knowledge is wisdom, that strength in the old by which they come to face ultimate concerns and thereby bequeath this strength to the next generation.[10]

II

The human problem of old age that I have been sketching is, then, the problem of courage. "Old age is not for sissies." Achieving the measure of wisdom and integrity needed for the task of closing life well is not easy. For the elderly have actually *seen* how badly life has kept the fair promises which youth held out. Weariness and discouragement, as well as a sense of futility in later years, can eventually deprive life of all color and warmth. Repeated failures tend to bring an abiding sense of limitation and deficiency. Even the experience of years, the one thing old people possess in abundance, tends to be discredited today, since modern technocratic society no longer believes that knowledge accumulates over the years but rather that it goes out of date.

Thus the materials, the occasions for courage come from old age itself. But what of the motivation for such courage? Does this also come from the simple fact that one is old? Or does it come rather from one's conviction that life is *worth* closing well, in the same way that it was worth beginning well and living through adulthood and middle age? The obstacle here, obviously, is that the source of this conviction can no longer be that evidence found earlier in life in the form of family, friends, and personal achievement. As one grows older, this conviction has to be based more and more on faith. This need not be a consciously religious faith. There is such a thing as faith in life itself, in the worth of one's own lived life, which must now be seen to the end because it is somehow valuable for its own sake and not for what it can usefully do. Let us examine more closely some of the implications of this faith.

The phenomenon of faith has received no little attention in recent years from both psychology and psychotherapy. Some regard it as a form of regression to be explained in terms of wish-fulfillment and instinctive drives, others as an intuition into an inherent intelligibility that lies beyond the limits of logic and reason. Freud saw the motivation of faith to lie in the terrifying effects of infantile helplessness which aroused the need for protection through love, and it would be difficult to deny this regressive moment in any type of faith. But, as William Meissner has noted, while the regression of faith reaches back to and draws upon basic instinctual forces, it concurrently transforms them into a new synthetic integration, a reassertion of that "basic trust" of which Erik Erikson speaks.[11] And Erikson himself writes that man "forgets that he achieved the capacity for *faith* by learning to overcome feelings of utter abandonment and mistrust."[12] Faith thus implies a capacity to trust, and it is through faith that trust finds its unique expression. In the case of the elderly such faith and trust have extraordinary importance because of the sense of loss and diminishment of self-esteem they experience. For these attack that fundamental narcissism essential to everyone's psychological well-being. Old people have to sustain loneliness, illness, frustration, abandonment, and the loss of love, and these griefs naturally tend to bring into play the mechanisms of substitution and sublimation by which the ego strives to recover its loss and to reconstitute its sense of self-esteem.[13] If an old person succeeds in this activation of faith and trust in life, then he or she will also find courage for the task of closing life well.

The Viennese psychiatrist Victor Frankl approaches this phenomenon of faith from a slightly different perspective. The central theme of his writings is that the most fundamental human drive is not sexual energy, as Freud said, nor the will to power, as Adler held, but rather the will to meaning. Thus what matters for the individual is not what he expects from life but what life expects from him. For it is life that asks questions of man. Each person is questioned by life daily and hourly, and is obliged to respond, to be responsible to life. "Life ultimately means taking the responsibility to . . . fulfill the tasks which it constantly sets for each individual."[14] Its meaning at any given moment, therefore, is not to be made but found. Frankl often quotes Nietzsche: "He who has a *why* to live can bear with almost any *how.*" Crises in the lives of the aging usually come because they suspect, after the rush of middle years, that they no longer possess a *why,* that all aspects of their life have become transitory. But, says Frankl, "the only really transitory aspects of life are the potentialities; the moment they are actualized, they are rendered realities; they are saved and delivered into the past, wherein they are rescued and preserved from transitoriness. For, in the past, nothing is irrevocably lost but everything irrevocably stored." Instead of possibilities, then, the old person has realities, "the full granaries of the past, wherein he has salvaged once and for all his deeds and his joys and also his sufferings. Nothing can be undone, and nothing can be done away with. I should say *having been* is the surest kind of being."[15]

Beginning with the same fundamental insight as Frankl, Karl Rahner has approached from a slightly different viewpoint this significance of time as an object of faith. One thing which can never be taken away from anyone, he says, especially the elderly, is what they were and hence continue to be. It is *becoming* that passes away, not that which *has become.* "What perishes is not the secret extract of life but the process of its preparation."[16] The old person is always working with the gains of his previous life and cannot act other than as the one who has lived this life. His past thus becomes an essential principle of his present and its acts, since this past is ultimately not "what happened" but what has become and been preserved. In this sense "eternity" is not to be conceived as yet another period appended to his life, added to it as a further prolongation of incalculable extent. For man does not bring his temporal mode of existence to an end by quitting it, but by compressing it, as it were, and bringing it with him in its totality as *his* time summed up and completed. Eternity is thus not the unlimited continuation of time but rather the fulfillment of time, the finality of what an individual has freely brought to be in time, namely his own concrete self. This is what Rahner calls the comfort of time: the belief that to close life well is also to attain oneself completely, with all that one has been and done, in strength as well as weakness.

But can one close life well with such remembered weakness? What will give the aged courage to live right to the end with all the guilt in their past? Rahner insists that, because the old are still "pilgrims of maturing freedom," even the moral evil they have embraced can still be retrieved and transformed. His reason is that evil action can only exist because it is more and something better than evil, for otherwise it would be pure nothingness. Some genuine self-fulfillment must come even from moral failure. Indeed, the deeper the failure, the more the individual involves and achieves his own person, and the more he must realize the possibility of his existence, even though his development is in a radically false direction. "The wretchedness and profound shamelessness of sin lived on in this real presence within it of the greatness of fulfilled human possibilities. The bravery, the prodigality of the heart, the courage to venture, and whatever else has to be carried out . . . all this could and should indeed have become reality even without guilt. . . . Yet this in turn does not alter the fact that it has become a reality in the guilt. And so it remains."[17]

Repentance is thus not escape but transformation. The life hidden
in the guilty deed must be embraced; only what was death in it
need be rejected. The years of old age are therefore rich in
possibilities to unlearn these failures of the past, to see through
one's self-deception and to widen the horizon of one's honesty.
Through repentance and wisdom losses of the time of guilt can
be made up. But courage to do so must come from a deepening
of faith. And this brings us now to faith in God, to the religious
dimension of faith in the worth of one's life.

III

I have said up to now that the human problem of old age is one
of courage. For in order to close life well a person has to achieve
some measure of wisdom and integrity and the price of this
achievement is high. Growing old is therefore a challenge to
believe enough in the worth of one's life to be able to support that
sense of loss, suppressed guilt, and lessening of self-esteem which
are endemic to the aging process. I have been speaking of such
faith in life as if it were unconnected with faith in God. No doubt
it is in a number of cases, but such people will be unusual, of very
strong character, whose clear sense of meaning in various stages
of their life has always been supportive and continues to be so in
their attitude toward life's ending. The faith of the majority of old
people, however, if it is to be supportive at all, must be rooted
in some transcendent value. "Human existence," says Victor
Frankl, "is essentially self-transcendence rather than self-actualiza-
tion."[18] Because the role of such belief is not to console or to
shield the old, but to give them courage, it will usually be perceived as an overcoming and will therefore focus upon those very
events that test courage. For everything reminds them of age: the
collapse of cherished values, the disappearance of friends, the
storing up of disappointments, the cruelty of the young, the
specter of loneliness. All around them people press ahead into
life; only they are condemned to feel no such urgency, to see no

particular importance for doing things one way or the other.[19]

By definition all these experiences are beyond one's control, and overcoming them consists in placing one's "basic trust" in a power which is also beyond one's control, where there is mystery, holiness, and love, and where life is more real than any we immediately perceive. Such a power we have traditionally called "God." Faith in "God" is in some form common to all religions, but in Christianity it is mediated by, as well as centered upon, the person of Jesus. To be a Christian obviously involves the acknowledgment of who Jesus is, a confession which, like all faith, is made without being able to offer a totally sufficient reason. But much more than such acknowledgment, to believe in Jesus means to trust him, and through him God. It is a commitment of one's life, not merely of one's intellect. The object of such trust is precisely the care of the Father which Jesus reveals, a care which extends the length of our lives. Except that when we are old there is a deeper perception of our *need* of such care.

Religion obviously serves best even for the elderly when it is interiorized as a way of life and not as a way of dying. Yet dying is nonetheless part of living, a truth of which old people are painfully aware. And while Christianity has always proclaimed the ultimate victory of all life in the resurrection of Jesus, it has never for this reason thought it morbid to meditate upon his passion. Indeed, it is precisely the redemptive value of Jesus' suffering and death that is the main source of strength for the Christian in his own time of trial. "We possess a treasure in earthen vessels," says St. Paul, "to make it clear that its surpassing power comes from God and not from us. We are afflicted in every way possible, but we are not crushed; full of doubts, we never despair. We are persecuted but never abandoned; we are struck down but never destoryed."[20]

This particular aspect of Christian life is especially pertinent to old age. For this is the time when we keenly feel what Pierre Teilhard de Chardin called the "passivities of diminishment." This phrase of his encompasses an area of his religious thought which says much about his outlook as a Christian. "The further one progresses in life," he wrote during the First World War, "the more one changes. And the more one changes the more one dies. This is precisely the law that governs our development."[21] But when he died at seventy-four he was still not satisfied with such facile summaries of physical evil's inevitability in an evolving universe. "For if our hearts are to yield without revolt to this harsh law of creation," he asked in his seventieth year, "is it not psychologically necessary that we discover, in addition, some positive value that can transfigure this painful waste in the process that shapes us, and eventually make it worth accepting?" He answers as a Christian that suffering, provided it be rightly accepted, can be transformed into an expression of love and a principle of action. "Suffering is still to be treated at first as an adversary and fought against right to the end; yet at the same time we must accept it in so far as it can uproot our egoism and center us more completely on God." Here is the ultimate meaning for old age of the cross of Christ: "a growth of spirit arising from a deficiency of matter, a possible Christification of suffering."[22]

This power of Christ to give life shows itself in a special way when, "as a result of his omnipotence impinging on our faith, events which show themselves experimentally in our lives as pure loss become an immediate factor in the union we dream of establishing with him."[23] In formal logic the notion of fullness excludes that of emptiness, but in real life this is not so at all. There are some fullnesses which continue and even become more perfect when they are emptied. Cavities essential to an organism, for example, usually appear in their primary stage in the shape of bulky wholes that eventually hollow themselves out. So it is with man. He is led by the very logic of his development to be transformed into something greater than himself. For the fruit to break open it must first be ripe and mature. Hence we must cherish "the 'emptinesses' as well as the 'fullnesses' of life—that is to say, its passivities and the providential diminishments through which Christ transforms directly and eminently into himself the elements and the personality which we have sought to develop for him."[24] And in a letter to a close friend: "In spite of the fundamental, prime, importance I've always been led to attribute to human effort and development, I realize that the soul begins to know God only when it is forced *really* to suffer diminishment within him."[25] One of the greatest of these is, of course, old age itself, "that slow, essential deterioration which we cannot escape . . . little by little robbing us of ourselves and slowly pushing us toward the end. . . . What a formidable passivity is the passage of time."[26]

Most important to his understanding of the role of diminishments, and especially significant to one's attitude toward old age, is what Teilhard has to say about Christian resignation. His concern here is the bitter contemporary reproach to Christianity for fostering passivity in the face of evil, an accusation "infinitely more effective at this moment in preventing the conversion of the world than all the objections drawn from science or philosophy." Christian submission to the will of God is in fact the very opposite of capitulation. Far from "weakening and softening the fine steel of the human will, brandished against all the powers of darkness and diminishment," such submission is precisely a resolute resistance to evil in order to reach through faith that "chosen point" where God is to be found. For God is not present simply anywhere at all in our passivities, but solely at that point of equilibrium between our tenacious endeavor to grow and the external opposition which finally overwhelms us. Only at this "chosen point" does our capacity to submit to God's will reach its maximum, for at that moment our submission necessarily coincides with the optimum of our fidelity to the human task. There is thus to be found in Christian resignation a truly human value, an acceptance of diminishment with faith, while at the same time never ceasing to struggle against it. "Leaving the zone of human successes and failures behind him, the Christian accedes, by an effort of trust in the greater than himself, to the region of suprasensible transformations and growth."[27]

IV

In *Monte Walsh*, William Fraker's film about the modern West, there is an aging cowhand whose way of life on the open range is slowly being destroyed by the advance of industrialization. A friend offers him a good job as a cowboy in a traveling circus, but he cannot bring himself to accept it. His friend asks why, and he answers: "I ain't spitting on my whole life." He is unable to act as if his past never existed; the loss of his livelihood is easier for him to bear than what he sees as an affront to his dignity. At the end of the film he faces an uncertain future with the renewed conviction that his life up to then has nonetheless had some significance and worth. A much more painful cry is wrung from Willy Loman at the end of Arthur Miller's *Death of a Salesman*. His son Biff taunts him: "Pop! I'm a dime a dozen, and so are you!" Willy shouts back in rage: "I am not a dime a dozen! I am Willy Loman, and you are Biff Loman!" Yet his sense of loss in old age is too deep, and finally he allows it to kill him.

What we have been exploring in this chapter is not only the inevitability of this loss but also the need for a new sense of life (the wisdom or integrity of Erikson) in order to sustain it with courage. This is a "sense" that one's life as a whole has been important enough to be now worth closing well. Such belief can be based upon the love of family and friends as well as upon remembered achievements, but for the Christian it must ultimately rest upon the religious conviction that one's life has been and still is important to God. Old age will make sense in the end only if life makes sense. "It is Margaret you mourn for," but only God knows why there is any Margaret in the first place. Eventually everyone begins to grow old and to be reduced to a narrowing space-time in which only a few things offer what Erikson calls "a firm whisper of confirmation." The strongest of these is trust in God's present protection and hope in his eventual triumph over the bereavement of death.

There is obviously a close relationship between these two diminishments of old age and death, with acceptance of one always involving acceptance of the other. But there is just as close a relationship between old age and growth, and this is too easily forgotten. The years of aging can in fact be very formative years. In *King Lear* Shakespeare depicts old age not as the end of life but as its truth, as a time when it is at last possible to see life as a whole, unclouded by wealth, honors, or passion, to deepen one's understanding and compassion for man's failure as well as to look in awe upon his glory. Lear's truth, however, is that he is narrow, obstinate, and domineering, overwhelmed by blind passions which eventually unhinge him from reality and turn his life into "a tale told by an idiot, full of sound and fury, signifying nothing." Contrast these lines from *Macbeth* with the following by the Psalmist:

> It is you, O Lord, who are my hope,
> my trust, O Lord, since my youth.
> On you I have leaned from my birth,
> from my mother's womb you have been my help.
> My hope has always been in you.
>
> My fate has filled many with awe
> but you are my strong refuge.
> My lips are filled with your praise,
> with your glory all the day long.
> Do not reject me now that I am old;
> when my strength fails do not forsake me. . . .
>
> You have burdened me with bitter troubles
> but you will give me back my life.
> You will raise me from the depths of the earth;
> you will exalt me and console me again.
> So I will give you thanks on the lyre
> for your faithful love, my God.[28]

Such prayer is very close to life, and in many ways the two are identical. For in each there is the same experience of need. The old still need to learn what is important and unimportant, how to forgive and be forgiven, how to leave everything in God's hands. If their "second childhood" is seasoned with wisdom, then it will not develop into a sanctioned period of childishness but rather bring that childlike conviction that all is one, that everything is under protection, that all will be well. Such an outlook allows the elderly to value much more their immediate experience, to receive the next moment as a gift, to "let go" of what tends to distract them from the richness of the present. They need no longer feel the same desire to wield power over others, to exercise their roles in society, or to plan what they must do to live better tomorrow. At rest before the God who loves them, they can face without panic the loss of their future, and can more easily call upon their resources for choices to be made here and now. Their weakness does not terrify them. With St. Paul they say "I am content with weakness. . . . When I am powerless, it is then that I am strong. . . . He said to me, 'My grace is enough for you, for in weakness power reaches perfection.' "[29]

The reader may perhaps be surprised at the tone of passivity with which I am ending this chapter. I have said almost nothing about those critical problems of old people today which require anything but passivity: the economic plight of so many, the pressing need to reform their public health care, the remedies to be sought in order to lessen their endemic isolation. Much less have we dealt with the difficulties of geriatrics. But the elderly are not the ones who can deal with such questions. This is the task of legislators responsible for public policy, like the U. S. Senate's Special Committee on Aging; or the officials who design those procedures for obtaining Social Security and Medicaid programs which demean the dignity and self-respect of the old; or the administrators of America's 23,000 nursing homes, that booming private industry which the aging fear so much and will do anything to avoid.[30] Interestingly enough, many of the new theories touching these issues seem to be more advanced in their application in Europe than in the United States.[31] But whatever the country, it is the person dealing with such theory or its application who ultimately shapes society's attitude and can either activate or assuage its uneasy conscience. Old people themselves cannot solve problems that are financial or medical. They cannot go on strike. They cannot help it if the young and healthy see them as disagreeable reminders of mankind's common end. Neither can they remedy their invisibility: the fault is not theirs that people do not see them in the same way that one sees a pretty girl or the driver at the wheel of a shiny car.

We have not touched upon any of these matters, important as they are. My concern from the start has been rather with how we think of our lives here and now in function of our own inevitable aging process. Such thinking on our part cannot be passive at all. For when we speak of human maturation (or growth in wisdom) we are not dealing with the same thing as the natural growth of flowers or plants. Human maturity is not a bonus that comes automatically with old age, but a dynamic process depending upon free and conscious decision throughout life. Concealed within each of us is a potential which only begins to develop as the physical body begins to fail. Deep-rooted aspects of our inner lives are frequently suppressed during the years we spend building up our families and social identity and developing our careers. The direction of personality from middle to old age should thus be one of increased inner orientation and increased separation from the environment, a certain centripetal movement which leads to greater consistency and less complexity. But such a direction has to be freely chosen, since our natural tendency is to resist it. "Whoever carries over into the afternoon the law of the morning," writes Jung, "must pay for doing so with damage to his soul just as surely as a growing youth who tries to salvage his childish egoism must pay for this mistake with social failure." He then adds pointedly, "But we must not forget that only a very few people are artists in life; that the art of life is the most distinguished and rarest of all the arts. Whoever succeeded in draining the whole cup with grace?"[32]

Yet this lack of grace can itself become the occasion for both growth in humility and the retaining of one's sense of humor. Humility comes when we see that by growing old and accepting inevitable debility we are in fact fulfilling our destiny. But humor is perhaps the greatest gift of all. When found in a man or woman of faith such humor is wonderful indeed. For it enables the possessor, as Romano Guardini has said, to carry everything into the boundless love of God, including the inadequate, the strange, and the weak, to hope for solutions when reason and effort can do no more, and to discern a purpose where earnestness and zeal have long since given up finding one. "Existence, to be sure, is what it is, and man what he knows himself to be. But God has a wonderful name, the Lord of Patience. God's divine patience rests upon his sovereign power and his love, and it can achieve what the world cannot."[33]

6

Death

While the negative aspects of old age are many, ranging from illness and dependency to the loss of wealth and social status, the most threatening of all is the slow coming of death. Death has therefore, like old age, become an object of an extraordinary amount of concealment. This is because our culture tends to be much more comfortable with lives which are one-dimensional—which ask only immediate questions of a technical kind and limit their horizons to mundane concerns of everyday living. To become concerned with death, on the other hand, is to cease to be one-dimensional, since the experience of death in any form always forces one to ask the meaning of life. For death contains within itself the whole mystery of the human creature. Indeed, this mystery seems to have become deeper in our own time precisely because our race knows so much more about itself. From history, depth psychology, biology, physics, and sociology we have amassed information unknown to earlier generations. Yet none of it really tells us much about ultimate things, like why we must live or why we must die. For such questions we still have no answers that satisfy, and so we humans continue to plumb our own mystery. Kurt Vonnegut sees this continuous searching to be man's uniqueness. He is cursed to inquire after purpose, whether he wants to or not. In *Cat's Cradle* people chant a calypso-psalm:

> Tiger got to hunt,
> Bird got to fly,
> Man got to sit and wonder, "Why, why, why?"
> Tiger got to sleep,
> Bird got to land,
> Man got to tell himself he understand.

Because death focuses upon this uniqueness in a most acute way, it has gradually become something of an obsession for moderns. Such obsession means that, while we are not yet able to live with the question of death, we nonetheless have a desperate need to do so, simply in order not to become less than rational.[1] The real problem, therefore, is not biological death but what precedes it, not what lies on the other side of death but what lies on this side of it, not the act of dying but the act of living. Nor should our effort be to dissipate the mystery of death with some facile orthodoxy, whether religious or some other, but rather to locate this mystery, to push the mind as far as it can go before it must end in that same reverence which we give to the mystery of life. Any religious discussion of death is thus concerned ultimately with reverence for a mystery. It must begin with what other disciplines say about death, but it cannot end there. For theology has a role no other discipline has, namely, to create room for human hope. My own theological approach here will be Christian, one which regards the death of a certain man as the fundamental salvific event of world history. But this theological understanding must be tested by the human experience as a whole. It is with this experience, then, that we shall begin, insofar as it tries to focus today upon the phenomenon of death. We shall then understand better the Christian effort to interpret this experience and to create room for expectation and hope.

I

I noted a moment ago that the contemporary experience of death has resulted in two basic responses, both equally strong: concealment and obsession. More than one observer has insisted that only the category of the sacred can bring these two curious phenomena together.[2] "Men are tempted to conceal death or to hold themselves enthralled before it only because they recognize death as an overmastering power before which all other responses are unavailing."[3] Societies of the past have all seemed able to give some explanation of the origin and meaning of death; only for ours is it an enigma. It threatens us so much that we try to reduce it to a mere biological fact, a communicable disease which occurs out of sight in the antiseptic atmosphere of hospitals or in faraway retirement centers for the elderly. One reason that war and the ever present atom bomb are such terrors is precisely because they force death upon us suddenly, in ways we cannot control. Desire for such control is most evidenced in those burial rituals, researched a decade ago by Jessica Mitford, in which funeral parlors become euphemistic "slumber rooms" and the death pallor of fashionably dressed corpses is covered up with "Nature-Glo—the ultimate in cosmetic embalming."[4]

Why such concealment? Because people today have become infinitely more sensitive to the nothingness of death, the complete cessation of human resources, their utter inability in death to be or do anything.[5] Ingmar Bergman's film, *Cries and Whispers,* is filled with just such an image of death, a terrifying void through which we must all pass and to which there must be total submission. At one point in the film the local pastor, who has known the dead woman since her childhood, prays at her bedside: "Pray for us who are left here on the dark earth. Lay your burden of suffering at God's feet and ask him to pardon us. Ask him to free us from our anxiety, our weariness, and our deep doubt. Ask him for a meaning to our lives." A very different kind of anguish is to be found in Dylan Thomas' commemoration of his father: "Do not go gentle into that good night. Rage, rage against the dying of the light." Paul Tillich believed that such reactions manifest an existential anxiety before nonbeing which belongs to human existence as such, although it is usually transformed into a simple fear of dying. "Insofar as it is fear, its object is the anticipated event of being killed by sickness or an accident, and thereby suffering agony and the loss of everything. Insofar as it is anxiety, its object is the absolute unknown 'after death,' the non-being which remains non-being even if it is filled with images of our present experience."[6] What can be done with such anxiety? Tillich's answer is what he calls "the courage to be," courage grounded in faith in life which says Yes to being without seeing anything concrete that could conquer nonbeing.

Here Tillich is not far from the thought of Martin Heidegger, for whom authentic living means the acceptance of one's finitude. This means an acceptance of death, since the human being is finite because he exists *unto* death. Death is the limiting condition of all his possibilities, whether regarding himself as a person or regarding what he dreams of accomplishing in his world. His sudden excitement at the discovery of his own technological prowess can be defended only by ignoring the inescapable fact that he is what Heidegger calls him, a "being-unto-death." If he does ignore this fact, then his perspective on life becomes purely technological and ceases to be rooted in history at all. For "death is not an event which puts an end to life, but . . . a part of life itself. It is not something occurring at the end of a man's life, but something always present, from the very beginning of life, as a constitutive element of existence. Thus death lies not in the future, but in the here and now. . . . It is thus seen not by looking ahead, but by re-flecting, i.e. looking back upon existence."[7] It is this "re-flection" upon death, this capacity in us to contemplate our own death, that makes this death a truly human event, uniquely distinctive in us and totally different from the death of animals and plants.

Following Heidegger's lead, Karl Rahner speaks of the "axiological" presence of death through the whole of life and underlines the importance of this for human freedom and moral decision. To evade this axiological presence is to flee from moral seriousness into triviality—to believe that good and bad decisions can always and easily be undone and a fresh start made in an unceasing circle of time which constantly repeats itself. Whereas, on the contrary, time is limited, and to choose freely means to sacrifice some value, to ignore some option, to reject one opportunity and seize upon some other. Insofar as life is irrevocable, these choices too are irrevocable. Freedom is thus not the power constantly to change one's course of action (which would hardly have much meaning or value), but rather the power to decide what is to be definitive in one's life, what one really *wants,* something *not* to be either superseded, revised, or replaced. At its deepest level, therefore, the exercise of freedom bears upon death, for death brings to an end that prolongation of temporal existence which prevents us from definitively determining the shape of our lives. Death gives true value to every fleeting and transitory moment of time by making it possible for the imperfect decisions made in these moments to become final and complete, of permanent validity, beyond all possibility of revision.[8]

The terror and mystery of death, then, which we moderns both avoid and revere, arise from the fact that dying in any form forces upon us an experience of nonbeing, of finitude, and of the full implications of our freedom. This means that a person who is aware that he is dying during the whole of his life is forced to be aware also of the way in which he is living. If death in man is obviously not a matter of mere biological death, then life also is not a matter of mere biological life, of breathing, eating, and sleeping, but rather of the *quality* of life. "What am I doing with my life?" To see death as an integral part of life is not to regret that one must die, but to fear that one may not be living. Religions have traditionally been concerned with ultimate meanings *of* life, but such meanings *of* life really tell a man or woman nothing unless they also enable them to discover meanings *in* life: values of love, of family, of moral character and creative human achievement. For without these any life is diminished. These meanings each must find for himself, for they will determine the quality of life, and it is this quality, however limited by human frailty, which will determine how we face the moment of death.[9]

Elizabeth Kübler-Ross, in a remarkable report of her work as a psychiatrist with dying patients, emphasizes again and again that a person who has found such meanings in life can usually accept death more easily.[10] Those who do not, inevitably have to go through the four painful stages of denial, anger, bargaining, and depression before coming to the final stage of acceptance, which many in fact never do reach. Nor does religious faith seem able to relieve the majority of this conflict and fear. What *does* relieve them is their relationships with family and friends who genuinely care for them, who can give them assurance that their lives have been of some significant value and that they will not be forgotten when they die. If there is no one to give such assurance, then the dying person is forced to look for a meaning in his past which he may never have searched for before. The data which Dr. Kübler-Ross and others have amassed is significant because it shows what happens when men and women are forced by illness not to stumble into death blindly, as does the animal, but to think about it in advance and cope with it in a way that is worthy of human dignity. For human death is much more mystery than fact, and when mysteries can no longer be concealed they can only be faced with either courage or despair.

II

What I have said thus far can be summarized by a text of Jung: "From the middle of life onward, only he remains vitally alive who is ready to *die with life.* For in the secret hour of life's midday the parabola is reversed, death is born. . . . The negation of life's fulfillment is synonymous with the refusal to accept its ending.

Both mean not wanting to live; not wanting to live is identical with not wanting to die. Waxing and waning make one curve."[11]

It is easier, of course, to give this advice than to help people follow it. It is easy also to assert that the Christian experience of death creates expectation and hope, and in many cases it actually does. But it is likewise true that dying, even for very religious people, can be a dark and frightening encounter. Remember Dr. Kübler-Ross' statement that the religious faith of many of her dying patients seemed to give them very little support.[12] Hence, as I have said earlier, simple assertions of a theoretical Christian orthodoxy do not really solve anything, least of all how to hope in the face of death. Affirmations like "physical death is only the prelude to our being raised up to an endless life of perfect fulfillment" are to be treated with the utmost caution. When taken over uncritically they are little more than the repository of our own projected fantasies, many of them unconscious.[13] My approach in this second part of our discussion, therefore, will be to compare what Christian faith says about death with man's actual experience of it. For unless Christianity keeps in touch with the impact death has upon man's desire for meaningful life, it will simply move, as it has so often in the past, from one facile triumphalism to another.

To begin with, as William Lynch has pointed out, Christians have to hold on to all the finite structures in human life along with their climax in death. It is pure romantic fantasy to declare the moment of death to be one of magnificence and energy whereas our experience tells us it is a moment of complete impotence and helplessness. Christian hope does not impose upon us any romantic burden of perpetual human strength, just as Christian faith does not force us to give up our human darkness. Neither faith nor hope take their form and outline from what we already are, but from what we are not.[14] Christianity therefore does not burden us with the hopeless project of not really dying, or of not really experiencing either the pain or darkness of death. What it does do is to explain why the acceptance of this darkness is so dreadful and difficult. Whatever may be the immediate human reason, Christianity asserts that the ultimate reason is that before God man is a sinner.

The point at issue here, it should be noted, is not at all the causal relationship between sin and death. With the discoveries of modern science Christianity has passed well beyond any idea of physical death as a penalty for sin. Death belongs to nature and therefore to human nature. The resources of life simply exhaust themselves. When the author of Genesis assures us that death has to do with sin, he means that a person with little experience of sin or selfishness would face death in a way very different from the rest of us. The reason, quite obviously, is that, for the Christian, God is the one responsible for the impermanence of life, and to face death is to face God. The selfish person fears death precisely because he is selfish and proud and shrinks from the endurance of anything that demands obedience or love or self-sacrifice. Death demands all three. It is required by our nature, yet we rebel against it, refusing to integrate it into our daily existence. In the end, of course, we must. That freedom of ours by which we open or close ourselves to interventions from outside us, must, whether we like it or not, be exercised totally and irrevocably in death. For in dying we are wholly subject to the control of God. Every possibility of autonomously ruling our own destiny is taken away from us. To the extent that we rebel against this finitude, everything appears to be taken from us by force. But to the extent that we overcome this selfishness and pride and accept this fall into helplessness, to that extent we yield ourselves to a mystery we cannot fathom, a mystery which Christianity calls God.[15]

Christian faith, then, has little to say about the existence of death but much to say about its acceptance. Death is a fall into the hands of a God who is our Father, but man's sinfulness shrouds this event in darkness and makes it an object of fear and dread. The Christian doctrine of the death and resurrection of Jesus does not remove this darkness, but proclaims instead that on its other side something of ourselves endures and maintains itself. The menace of dying, which seems to throw a final boundary around man's greatest contributions of love and freedom and fidelity, must therefore confront the Christian affirmation that the purpose of existence is precisely to make such contributions, because somehow they are destined to last forever on the other side of this boundary. In other words, final victory is on the side of life. And this victory, for the Christian, is to be seen concretely in the person of Jesus.

Jesus himself was continually making references to his death, and it seems to have conditioned both his preaching and his way of life. His call for decision on the part of anyone who followed him had such urgency because death must come to every man. There is great significance, moreover, in the fact that, notwithstanding the cult of splendor which has characterized the Christian church in history, it is still the crucifix that remains the most common and most popular representation of Jesus. For not only did he die, but, as the Christian credal formula states, he descended into hell, into the realm of the dead; he was actually in the *state* of death. Nor was this state passively endured as something inflicted from without; Christian conviction has always been that Jesus seized hold of death, grappled with it, made it his own. This is why, in Christian tradition, his death has always been seen to be redemptive: because his total acceptance of ultimate darkness and dread was precisely a total negation of human selfishness and sin, a free transfer of Jesus' existence to the Father in obedience, hope, and love: "Father, into your hands I commend my spirit."[16] Over the centuries Christians have sought in their sacramental system to give visible form to this redemptive death and so enable all Christians to share in it. St. Paul says that in baptism a person is buried with Christ, becomes like him in his death, and in this way dies to sin.[17] The Eucharist too has always been understood as the continuously renewed celebration of Jesus' death; indeed, is believed to make that death somehow actually present, so that in announcing it the Christian announces his own death as well, a death he hopes will be taken up into the victory of life.[18] "Continually we carry about in our bodies the dying of Jesus," says St. Paul, "so that in our bodies the life of Jesus may also be revealed."[19]

It is therefore all the more extraordinary that this continuous affirmation of the death of Jesus should be accompanied in the Christian message by an equally strong and almost blatant proclamation that Jesus was raised from the dead, is now glorified and living with God, and that, as St. Paul says, we too "if we have died with him, shall also live with him."[20] The New Testament, in other words, knows of no human life which is not worthy to be definitive. What knowledge do we have of such existence beyond death? None, if by knowledge we mean scientifically verifiable evidence. But nobody in fact lives his life by such evidence, since it would merely allow him to classify objects, and forbid him any experience either of art or beauty or friendship or love. Peter Berger, who has recently taken a rather dim view of religion as mostly human projection, admits nevertheless that within such projection there are inklings of transcendence, "rumors" as he calls them: experiences of beauty, of play, and especially of love. In these experiences man seems to escape his finitude for brief moments and to feel an extraordinary sense of fulfillment.[21] Human love, for example, is quite shameless in hoping for immortality, and believes against all evidence that it will not be affected by death. The free act of moral decision as well as true moral goodness are also experienced as somehow absolutely valuable, beyond any apparent hopelessness or futility in time. We all know that such a thing as "psychological" truth exists and that it is just as operative in our attitudes and decisions as any "physical" truth. "Truth and fact well up in our lives in ways that exceed verbal formulation," writes William James apropos of religious experience. "There is in the living act of perception always something which glimmers and twinkles and will not be caught and for which reflection comes too late."[22] This is obviously the type of experience that overpowered the disciples on Easter. They clearly could not handle it with rational discourse. The only appropriate words they could find to express the new reality of Jesus was the suggestive and metaphorical expression "resurrection from the dead"—it was like rising from sleep, but in this case to a life which was totally new.

The Christian's hope, then, that the whole of his being somehow endures and maintains itself through death, while not based on the verifiable evidence of science, is yet consistent with the special kind of knowledge we have from certain types of human experience. Like human desire, the object of Christian hope is fulfillment, but—unlike desire—hope is expectancy in face of a future which is ultimately unknown and totally beyond our imagination. "Eye has not seen," says St. Paul, "ear has not heard, nor has it so much as dawned on man what God has prepared for those who love him." And again he says, "Hope is not hope if its object is seen."[23] All images of this future life must therefore be spoken in metaphor. Not to understand this, to believe that Christianity knows anything at all about the future life it announces, is to make Christian faith and hope ridiculous and incredible. Hope looks for the radically new beyond death, a fulfillment utterly beyond our power to conceive. The only thing Christianity can say about the resurrection of the flesh is that what happened to Christ will also happen to us, to the extent that our lives have been genuinely worth while. We will come before God face to face, in absolute nearness to absolute mystery. And in that nearness we shall be forever what we have become in our lives and have ratified in death.

III

I have said up to now that the human problem of death is not so much its existence as its acceptance as part of one's life, not so much its destruction of life as its ability to influence those free moral decisions which determine life's quality. Christianity in its turn is concerned with explaining why acceptance of death is so difficult, and with presenting the person of Jesus both as model of such acceptance and as hope for the ultimate victory of life:

Jesus is God's pledge that on death's other side he will somehow restore human life and gloriously transform whatever quality it has been able to achieve. A nagging question still remains, however. If death is a natural part of that human biological process for which God is responsible, why should there be a reversal of this process after death? Is the resurrection to be understood as an afterthought on the part of the creator, a rectification of his own biological world, arbitrarily granted to the human species and to no other? Christians cannot avoid this question by appealing to the immortality of the soul, for such natural immortality in the Platonic sense was inconceivable for those who announced the resurrection.[24] For St. Paul, for example, man's spirit is just as mortal as his body: it dies through sin. God's forgiveness in redemption does not set free in this spirit (or "soul") some natural life it already has, but rather recreates a life which sin has completely lost. Hence the message of the New Testament does indeed seem to be that God reverses through redemption what he has done through creation: the whole of man dies and the whole of man is given new life in and through the risen Christ.[25]

Now the Christian today can hardly be content with such an understanding of resurrection. He really has to be able to point to a much more intrinsic connection between death as a life process and the undoing of this death announced by Christianity. Otherwise we should have to say that there is no relationship whatsoever between what God is doing biologically and what he is doing through Christ. The Christian today must likewise ask why it is that man alone, among at least two million existing biological species, has such difficulty in accepting death and integrating it into his life process; why he claims that death makes *his* life absurd but claims no such thing for the death of other forms of life? Is his constant refusal to accept his finitude really a rebellion *against* life, or is it rather an assertion of what human life must actually be? And if so, why?

Questions such as these troubled Pierre Teilhard de Chardin most of his life. What he asked as a Christian was whether there was anything in the life process, as we know it scientifically, which could make Christian expectation of an afterlife believable. His answer led him to analyze in some detail the relationship between what he called the "two complementary expressions of the arrow of time." On the one hand there is the law of entropy, the second law of thermodynamics, discovered over a century ago by physics, which says that the quantity of unusable energy in the universe is constantly increasing. This means that all matter of its nature tends to become diffused, sliding irresistibly downward, so that eventually, at some remote point in time, there will be no more energy to use: all activity will have stopped, except that of atoms vibrating in the icy darkness of space. In biology, on the other hand, we have an analysis of the phenomenon of life, revealing a long chain of composites extending from the electron to man by way of proteins, viruses, and bacteria, which clearly seems to be moving in the opposite direction, namely, toward an extraordinary degree of complexity and arrangement. This phenomenon of life, Teilhard says, although a relative newcomer to the universe and occupying an incredibly small volume of space, manifests itself nevertheless as having developed in the very heart of the flow of entropy precisely as an eddy, as a countercurrent. In other words, while the behavior of matter is totally predictable, the behavior of life in the midst of matter has, over millions of years, been totally unpredictable. Entropy and life, two properties of matter as we have come to know it, the one pulling backward, the other forward, the one a dissipation of energy, an unfolding or granulating of matter, the other an increase of energy, a complexification of matter, a tendency in matter to arrange or center itself around growth in consciousness. In entropy we have a descent toward ever more probable zones of disintegration, whereas in life we discover an ascent toward ever more improbable zones of interiority and, in the case of man, personality.[26]

It is this phenomenon of man, of course, that fascinates Teilhard—this most recent arrival in the universe as we know it, with powers of reflection, self-awareness, and—most significantly—

death-awareness. The human creature alone has been able to ask whether this growth of life in the midst of entropy, and more particularly he himself, are indeed no more than a flash on the cosmic time scale, a momentary and accidental by-effect of the general downward movement of entropy. For if he is only this, then what is to be made of his perennial concern with death, his constant resistance to it, his charge that such an end to his life makes that life absurd? The fact is, writes Teilhard, that "through the germ of consciousness born upon its surface, the earth, our perishable earth which itself looks ahead to absolute zero, has brought forth into the universe a need, henceforth irrepressible, not only not to die, but actually to save completely whatever earth has developed in complexity and consciousness, whatever is *best* in the world. It is through human consciousness, genetically linked to a planet whose years are clearly numbered, that evolution proclaims its demand: either it must be irreversible, or let it not go on at all!"[27]

Why should the human creature make such a demand? Because, according to Teilhard, the development of life, that extraordinary phenomenon in the midst of universal entropy, is now his responsibility. If nothing of what we create, or even more, if all that is best in what we create, is not seen as somehow winning through the disintegration of matter, then evolution must certainly be struck at its very heart by self-disgust and automatically come to a halt. For, as Teilhard is never tired of repeating, *we* are evolution. Thus, in his analysis, life gives rise to reflection, reflection to foresight, and foresight to a demand for some escape from death. His postulate here, it should be noted, is the impossibility of the universe disappointing the consciousness it has engendered if that consciousness is to be able to function at all. The energy of human reflection is irreversible because it *has* to be so in order for man to continue to act. Teilhard was well aware, of course, that many serious thinkers challenged this postulate. He himself cited Albert Camus and Norbert Wiener, and we might add today the name of the French geneticist, Jacques Monod.[28] But Teilhard also felt that eventually mankind would come to a true consensus on the truth of this postulate. "Today," he said, "ninety-nine percent of men, perhaps, still fancy that they can breathe freely this side of an unbreakable death-barrier—provided it is thought to be sufficiently far away. Tomorrow . . . a kind of panic claustrophobia is going to seize mankind at the mere thought of finding itself hermetically sealed up inside a closed universe."[29]

What Teilhard is trying to get his readers to accept as plausible, therefore, is the hypothesis that man can escape from entropy and death precisely *through* entropy and death. All life, including human life, is clearly subject to entropy. But if in man's case this biological end is final, with no emergence at all on the other side, then no one would ever shoulder the burden of human advance. Survival after death is thus manifest in dedication to life. Teilhard's analysis of human psychic interactivity is aimed at showing that such an escape would take place not outwardly, in space and time, but inwardly, in depth and through a paroxysm of consciousness, a using up of all man's physicochemical resources.[30] In other words, death would be the location of the ultimate interiorization of both individual and species. "To be cosmically shut up, all together, in the universe," Teilhard asks, "to be shut up as individual atoms, each on his own, each inside himself: must we accept that such is the tragedy of man's condition?"[31] His answer is clearly No: given two theoretically possible ways of looking at reality, the one leading to asphyxiation and paralysis, the other, on the contrary, engendering a taste for life and an impetus for action—between two such interpretations of the universe no hesitation can be allowed. To the objection that the second interpretation, however appealing, may not be true, Teilhard answers that there is a way to confirm it; there is a way for man to know that he can *in fact* escape entropy and death. "Here there comes out into the open," he says, "not simply the philosophical problem of immortality but . . . the question . . . of a revelation."[32]

It is not to our purpose here to develop at length the role of

Christianity in Teilhard's understanding of death. This I have done elsewhere.[33] Suffice it to say that it confirmed for him, through its belief in the historical death and resurrection of Jesus, the truth of his own analysis of evolution. For in the person of Jesus it can be *seen* that human transformation does indeed come from the breakdown of matter. It is Jesus' free acceptance of death that has given it, physically, the value of a metamorphosis.

> The great victory of the creator and redeemer, in the Christian vision [writes Teilhard in *The Divine Milieu*] is to have transformed what is itself a universal power of diminishment and extinction into an essentially life-giving factor. God must in some way or other make room for himself, hollowing us out and emptying us, if he is finally to penetrate into us. And in order to assimilate us into him, he must break the molecules of our being so as to recast and re-model us. The function of death is to bring about this opening up of our inmost selves. . . . It will put us into the state organically needed if the divine fire is to descend upon us. And in that way its fatal power to decompose and dissolve will be harnessed to the most sublime operations of life. What was by nature empty and void, a return to bits and pieces, can, in every human existence, become fullness and unity in God.[34]

We said at the start that any religious discussion of death must ultimately be concerned with reverence for mystery. From the Christian's point of view this mystery centers upon the human experience of selfishness and sin as well as upon the person and role of Jesus. The modern avoidance of death, both socially and psychologically, is really a denial by man of his sinfulness. For to accept death as part of one's life means that one has to integrate it into those free moral decisions which determine life's quality. And this cannot be done without an acceptance of one's finitude and need of help, without an acknowledgment of moral weakness at the heart of one's freedom. In other words, to live with death a person needs to hope that he is not autonomous and alone. For a Christian such hope comes from the redemptive strength of Christ's death and resurrection, which is his pledge that what he is and does will not in the end disappear. The work of Teilhard de Chardin, in its turn, is one Christian's attempt to make credible such belief in life after death by focusing upon belief in life before death. As a scientist he believed he saw in the phenomenon of man an energy at work which would ultimately counteract the pull of entropy. This energy is man's zest for life, driving him to pursue to the very end the forces of the evolutionary process. It is therefore right for man to die, but only if he has not given in to boredom or apathy, only if he has actually used up all the energy that life has given him, only if he has sought for *more-being* and has not settled for mere *well-being*. This, as he says, is the Christian spirit: "the spirit of service and of giving; man struggling like Jacob to conquer and attain a supreme center of consciousness which calls him; the evolution of the earth ending in an act of union."[35]

Are there any conclusions we can draw at the end of this effort we have made to reverence a mystery? Three, I think. First, the language we have inherited to talk about death no longer says what we think and feel about it. This is especially true of the language of Christian orthodoxy, which is still used almost automatically in time of grief, but which in fact has tended to neglect empirical experience in favor of neat intellectual formulas. Whereas, as Abraham Heschel has said, the roots of ultimate insights are to be found not on the level of discursive thinking, but on the level of wonder and radical amazement, in the depth of awe, in our sensitivity to mystery. Hence our second conclusion that Christian hope in resurrection after death will have meaning for us only to the extent that we have some inkling of resurrection now, some experience of fullness of life, of self-discovery, love, or creativity. For to profess mere theoretical belief in the resurrection without witnessing to it in one's life is to have already buried it. This means that the Christian's expectation that God will finally answer the riddle of his existence must be integrated into a human acceptance of all the problems of that existence. Finally, as we said in the beginning, because death somehow contains the whole of man's mystery, it inevitably asks us for our identity: Who am I? The challenge of death is a challenge to what I am doing with my life. Ultimately this is a far more pressing question than what God will do with me after death, which is, after all, God's concern. The best Christian teaching about death has therefore always been teaching about life. To the extent that we know who we are and have reached the point where we can take moral responsibility for our lives, to that extent we are also ready for death and, as Jesus said, not very far from the Kingdom of God.

7

Christ

In the preceding chapters I have made an effort to situate some fundamental human experiences within the ambit of Christian faith. I have not dealt directly with the question of transcendence, yet implicitly it has provided the context for everything said. The various analyses have had as their major supposition that an opening to the transcendent, always at the heart of Christian belief, is now also becoming an essential factor in modern man's self-understanding. For the more he grows in autonomy and responsibility, the more he becomes aware of himself as contingent and of large areas of his life as resistant to control. Meaning tends continually to escape him; the anguish of living tends more and more to wear him down. Just as at the Renaissance there was the gradual recognition that the world was not totally sacral, so now there is the growing suspicion that neither is it totally secular. Some relationship, in other words, must exist between these two axes of the real. For the Christian the model of this relationship is the person of Jesus. This is why over the centuries the central problem of Christology has always been to understand how Jesus is both secular and sacral, how he can be completely man yet at the same time so completely the presence of God that St. Paul could say "God was in Christ reconciling the world to himself."[1]

More exactly, perhaps, Christology has tended to be a study of how Christians at various periods of history have come to think and speak about Jesus in ways very different from that of the New Testament. The reason for this perennial need to use words not used by Jesus himself is that God, and therefore his Christ, can only be known in relation to a particular world in which men live. Any self-revelation on his part which lies outside a given sphere of human existence simply cannot be heard. Hence what makes our knowledge of Jesus what it is are the specific cultural factors that make our world what it is; changes in one's human experience inevitably have their effect on one's religious experience. This conviction, it should be noted, is not an effort merely to accommodate religious affirmations to current psychological reality structures or to make public opinion the ultimate criterion of whether or not to accept a datum of faith; it is rather an effort to question anew the biblical witness to Jesus, which arises from our peculiar difficulty in speaking about him in our contemporary world. The questions we ask simply could not have been asked by a former generation of Christians, because they were living in their world, not ours. Nor can the Scriptures satisfy our questioning immediately, since their message was directed to men whose inquiry was quite different. "The Gospel does not answer questions that are not asked. Every generation asks the Gospel its own questions from the context of its own life. . . . The answer the Gospel gives us will therefore be new, but at the same time also *evangelical*. This presupposes that we should be ready . . . to change, extend or correct our questioning in the light of Scripture and biblical interpretation given during the church's whole history."[2]

The theme of this final chapter then is that, for a Christian today, to ask about the meaning of humanity is to ask about the meaning of Jesus, but to talk about Jesus will make sense only within the context of the Christian's own self-understanding. The Christological problem is thus one aspect of the larger problem of God. One thing learned from the meteoric rise of the "death of God" movement in the 1960s is the futility of speaking about God in language no longer understood by the average person. A similar difficulty is now being faced by theologians in attempting to articulate the significance of the divine and human as these exist in Christ. Nor does the sore spot lie in the correct interpretation of what the New Testament and tradition say about Jesus (though this must obviously not be neglected); it lies rather in the relationship of this primary data to the religious experience of men and women today. For it is always out of the present that we understand the past, and unless our present experience becomes an integral part of Christological inquiry there is danger that the inquiry itself, however seriously pursued historically, will be of no consequence whatsoever either to theology or to the contemporary Christian.

I

What hovers in the background of the general upheaval in society today, as I have said in earlier chapters, is the specter of a dehumanized world, the threat of the impersonal against persons. Technology is often made the scapegoat here, but in reality the difficulty lies not so much in technology as in its unquestioned supremacy in so many lives and the seeming insensitivity of large numbers to the rights and emotional needs of their fellow citizens. "Judgments of skill, competence, and effectiveness have replaced usefulness, beauty and relevance to human needs as criteria of worth; instrumental values have replaced final purposes; and cognitive skills have replaced virtuous character as standards of human value."[3] The problem is therefore not machines but overidentification with them, symbolized most strikingly perhaps by the astronaut: the mechanical expert whose computer-guided efficiency makes him as interchangeable as any part of the mechanism he pilots aloft. Integral to this symbol is the rule of will, calculation, and control, and absent from it are any of the desires of youth today for interpersonal feelings, fantasy, spontaneity, and play. The possibilities we now possess of genetic control merely confirm youth in the conviction voiced by C. S. Lewis that our power over nature is really the power of some people over other people, with nature as their instrument.

Gilbert Chesterton once said that alligators have no difficulty being alligators, but men always seem to have had difficulty in trying to be men. The present tension between the humanist and technological orientations must be seen as a tension between two different modes of being human, both of which hold promise of future triumph as well as future disaster. Hence the insistence of people like Erik Erikson that they must be kept in tension, so that one set of emphases will tend to counteract the dangers inherent in the other. This tension, moreover, is precisely a manifestation of that perennial desire in our hearts for self-transcendence. As such it must be recognized as a tension between two faith commitments. The struggle of the humanist is to overcome, not so much technology as the *deity* of technology, something he sees threatening the dignity of the person and his desire for community. He is haunted by reports of genetic manipulation, sperm banks, and other nightmares. The commitment of technological man, however, is no less one of faith, though in the last decade that faith has been badly shaken by the realization that man's knowledge is greater than his wisdom to manage it, and that his exploitation of the world may mean that our race will eventually commit suicide.[4] Nor is it an accident that those who call for a change of consciousness today use all the terminology of religious conversion. For the crisis man faces is in its deepest sense religious. From a Christian point of view this means it must be seen also as Christological, since Jesus is the way that God is human.

Historically what has generated fresh departures in the understanding of Christian revelation has not been the abstract preference for pluralism in theology, but insight into a given human situation that generates the passion to elucidate and communicate. "Vital theology does not emerge when a new generation takes up the leftovers from the problem supply. It is and always has been born out of the agony of faith and understanding precipitated by crisis."[5] Up to now what I have suggested is that our own crisis is inextricably bound up with a new search for a transcendent meaning for man. In the Christian context, however, any such new experience of transcendence must immediately open the way to a new experience of Christ. If it is genuine, this experience will in turn reflect that of the New Testament, namely of a Christ who promises and actually accomplishes something new, who justifies sinners, upsets all rigid schemes of order, unsettles the self-satisfied, and guarantees a future to the oppressed. Hence I suggest that the direction in which Christology should be moving today can be glimpsed by a closer examination of the Christ experience present in three interrelated areas in modern life: those of youth culture, ecology, and Black liberation. Let us briefly look at each of these, noting as we do that none of them has any significant relationship to religion in the institutional sense.

What one notices in the first area is the link now being forged between prayer, celebration, and play, a link frequently identified with the person of Christ. Certainly young people, in revolting against a secular and materialistic society, are looking for religious meaning in life, whether this be through mysticism or through ritual. The rock opera *Jesus Christ Superstar* was a striking example of this current reaction to an overcerebralized Christology. Whatever one's personal taste regarding the music, the lyrics can in fact become genuine prayer as well as an expression of groping faith: "Jesus Christ superstar, do you think you're what they say you are? . . . We all know you are news—but are you king? king of the Jews?" Or consider the extraordinary line in Jesus' Gethsemane prayer to the Father: "Show me there's a reason for your wanting me to die. You're far too keen on where and how and not so hot on why." The mysterious magnetism of Jesus is perhaps best revealed in the identical reactions to him of Mary Magdalene and Judas: "I don't know why he moves me. He's a man, he's just a man." To this Mary adds: "He scares me so. I want him so. I love him so." While Judas adds a question: "When he's cold and dead will he let me be? Does he love me too? Does he care for me?"

Young people likewise perceive more clearly than their elders that, as Harvey Cox has pointed out, there is something of the harlequin in Jesus. This approach carries a religious significance hardly appreciated by the institutional church. Yet to the extent that it is meaningful, one's relationship to Jesus does take on, as Cox suggests, the character of conscious play and comic equivocation. "Only by assuming a playful attitude toward our religious tradition can we possibly make any sense out of it. . . . Christ the clown signifies our playful appreciation of the past and our comic refusal to accept the specter of inevitability in the future."[6] This same blend of celebration, prayer, and play has also become an integral part of the Eucharistic liturgy as this is understood by youth today. They are indeed searching for Christ, but the Christ they find is someone very human. They see his total acceptance of life, his willingness to plunge into a destiny at once mysterious, ironic, and hopeful, as proof that risk is needed to be fully human, that "God's foolishness is wiser than human wisdom, and God's weakness stronger than human strength."[7]

A second area of concern today, that of ecology, would at first sight seem hardly to contain a Christ experience. Yet the environmental crisis has raised the whole question of the trustworthiness of the life-process in which man is involved. This question is very much open at present and the answer genuinely in doubt, for it is not at all evident that we intend to use responsibly the resources of nature around us. Indeed, descriptions of inevitable disaster from our present treatment of the environment can be grounds for depression and despair rather than for action. Christianity, moreover, has clearly played a part in all this, in so far as it has fostered an "otherworldly" outlook in people themselves and promoted at the same time the lordship theory over nature, according to which the human species is free to do whatever it likes.

Even the current Christian interest in festivity and celebration just discussed is focused much more on human experience and interiority than upon our responsibility for the world of nature. Hence the religious grounding for our outlook has to be completely rethought. For the problem is not what man must do, but whether he will have the asceticism actually to do it. Technology can easily be employed to deal effectively with the threat of ecological disaster, but the sacrifice which this will demand in money, loss of comfort, changes in living standards—such sacrifices are very far from current thoughts and plans. An extraordinarily strong motivation is needed to change this, and such motivation simply has to be ethical and religious. In Christian terms this means rethinking the role of asceticism in Christian life, and especially the image of Christ as one who lived for others. It means that Christians must experience a new call of Christ to sacrifice present happiness for the future good of the species, since it was for this species that Jesus died on the cross.[8]

Finally, the thoughtless violation of environment must inevitably force us to face more sharply the deeper question of our thoughtless violation of each other. Just now the phenomenon known as Black theology is recasting the whole problem of Christ by seeing this violation with blinding clarity and by insisting that moral outrage has its ultimate warrant in Christian revelation. "Jesus Christ, the Incarnate One," writes James Cone, "takes upon himself the oppressed condition so that all men may be what God created them to be. He is the Liberator par excellence, who reveals not only who God is and what he is doing, but also who we are and what we must do about human oppression. It is not possible to encounter this man and still remain content with human captivity."[9] To assess theologically the divine presence in the world, then, means to analyze the struggle for Black liberation, since Black theology believes that Christ himself is participating in this struggle. In Chapter 2 we saw why over the centuries the Christian church, which always advocated transformation in personal life, was never really open to such change in political and social life. This is the reason that American churches have generally tended to support the system rather than those Blacks who in rage and protest reject it as irrational. Yet in such Black visibility, says Gibson Winter, "the American system meets a transcendent judgment from within. At the heart of American urbanization arises a power which cannot be managed, controlled, put in its place, assimilated to the system."[10] The question being asked is whether there is any Valuer of human action, any ultimate Judge independent of the white man's value structure of prestige and success. In the New Testament the significance of the liberation preached by Jesus is that he ties it to a reality other than the human. It may even be said that "strictly speaking there is no revelation of hiddenness taking place in him, but acknowledgment of that Valuer who is always unconcealed to man as Judge and Liberator, and who does not play hide-and-seek with him. The hiding is done by man."[11]

The three areas I have just discussed, those of youth culture, ecology, and Black liberation, raise the question of their common denominator. I suggest that the Christ experience in each is one of hope: that outlook which sees the present as linked both to the historical Jesus and to the future fulfillment of his promises. The Christ of risk, the Christ of asceticism, the Christ of liberation, these three also manifest the conviction that hope is not simply waiting. In fact the Christ experience today underlines the futility of waiting, for if we cannot escape from the forces that tend to dehumanize us, then life is indeed absurd. The utopian outlook thus becomes a necessary part of the reality of Christian faith, insofar as a capacity for utopia is inherent in man's nature. This hope, however, is not a wish for what is imaginable; it is an effort to give historical reality to what is believed through faith *to be real*. Nowhere is this more clear than in the liturgical celebration of the Christian mystery. All the thirst of modern man for transcendent meaning is satisfied through the symbolic signing both of Christ's presence and his absence. In speech, gesture, and song we proclaim that the future Kingdom of God is now present in mystery and that the meaning of Jesus has become the meaning of our own life story. The Christian who searches for Christ through the aspirations of youth, through a reverence for nature, through the struggle of Blacks, such a Christian not only holds in tension the humanist and the technological orientations in our culture; he also fosters a new tension between politics and Christian eschatology. A situation is thus slowly being created in which the moral teaching of the New Testament can operate more fruitfully. All of which raises a much more fundamental question, namely, how the Christ who fosters this experience can be understood in such a way that his transcendence will appear as a model and a strengthening of our own efforts to transcend the cultural situation in which we find ourselves.

II

Jesus needs to be seen today as the supreme exemplification and model of the God-man relationship, the one who precisely in his humanity was able to transcend our world and become the transparent source of God's activity and presence among us. This is in fact reflected in all that Jesus does and says in the gospels. Like us he had passions and temper, was intolerant, anxious, and fearful, even wept. He became on occasion hungry, tired, and disillusioned. His followers saw all this, accepted him as he was, yet put their faith and trust in this carpenter's son because there was obviously also something very different about him. Eventually, after the resurrection, they confessed him as Lord, *Kurios,* in the earliest and shortest of the Christian confessional statements, thereby proclaiming that in him they found God defined. But as Robert McAfee Brown has noted, they were likewise proclaiming that in him they found themselves defined; in him they saw not only who God is but who they were meant to be. Their Christology, in other words, was at root an anthropology, since the divine presence in Jesus showed them the goal toward which all humankind is moving. This divinity of Jesus, moreover, was known to them only through his humanity and contained no message or benefit apart from his manhood. The pages of the New Testament make it obvious that Jesus is a man in the fullest sense, and that, precisely by being the man he was, he made God present in a unique way. This is why, as centuries passed, Christians could write much longer creedal statements in order to clarify for themselves how Jesus is truly God and truly man.

The most famous of these statements was formulated in 451 at the Council of Chalcedon by churchmen with very different preoccupations from those of the New Testament authors. One of the movements of the time which they feared was Adoptionism, which in its crudest form said that God simply used or adopted the man Jesus as his instrument and agent, and that therefore what was God in him was quite separate from what was man. Aside from the fact that the New Testament knew nothing of such duality, this position made it extremely difficult to explain how Jesus is identical with God. Along with this fear went a very strong influence from the Greek conviction that what did not change was superior to what did change, and that what was perfect was unrelated to transition. Hence the natural tendency at the Council to downplay development in Jesus and to erase the clear New Testament emphasis upon the qualitative difference in him after the resurrection: as the Son of God, Jesus somehow had to remain the same at all points in his life. There was, in other words, as John Robinson notes, the general assumption that to begin with an unqualified stress upon "true man" must eventually lead to a qualified stress upon "true God"; the danger in insisting that Jesus was *completely* human was that people would think him to be *merely* human. Using the framework of current Greek philosophy, therefore, Chalcedon elaborated a Christology of "descent" with a formula which stated that Jesus was one divine "person" with two "natures," that of God and that of man.

There has long been a general feeling among Protestant theologians, shared recently by a number of Roman Catholics, that serious problems exist today with this Chalcedonian formula.

"We do not serve the truth," writes Norman Pittenger, "nor do we honor our ancestors in the faith, when we fall back upon their precise phrasing and repeat in parrot-fashion their ideas, while all the time we know quite well that things are no longer the same as they were in their particular period of history. This is not responsible theology, even if some may wish to call it by the honored name of 'orthodoxy.' It is only repetitious theology."[12] In point of fact Chalcedon has over the years created the popular impression that we do not really have a man in Jesus at all but merely a human nature; he *appeared* to be a man but in fact was God just acting as a man.[13] Such a concept did relatively little damage to basic Christian faith only because the humanity of Christ was continually attracting attention through popular piety, best illustrated on the Roman Catholic side by the cult of the Sacred Heart. In recent years, however, the widespread acquaintance with the New Testament and the results of biblical criticism have resulted in a tendency of the average Christian to reject Chalcedon as unintelligible, since the transcendence it enunciates for Christ seems like a transcendence of God from some other world and not a transcendence of man in our own. The Council's assumption of a static Jesus, unchanged and somehow glorified from the start, simply cannot handle the contemporary faith experience. For us, Jesus' divinity must be perceptible in his humanity itself: "He who sees me, sees the Father." As Edward Schillebeeckx has said, the mystery must be neither beyond nor beneath the man Jesus, but in his being-man itself. "The divine, remaining what it is, is perceived in the measure of the human. . . . Thus we do not have present a man, Jesus, in whom is realized the presence of God which is *distinct* from him. The man Jesus himself *is* the presence of God."[14]

The term "person," as used by Chalcedon, also makes it extremely difficult for the popular mind to experience Jesus as a flesh-and-blood creature like ourselves. The Council took over the word from the trinitarian theology of the day where it designated what there were three of in God. By contrast, our use of "person" can find only one in God, since for us the word refers to a personal center of action with a finite self-consciousness and freedom. To deny that Jesus is a human person is thus tantamount to denying that he is a man. Hence it is much more intelligible today to think of the subjectivity of Jesus as a human subjectivity and to locate the mystery of the incarnation in the fact that this human subjectivity belongs completely to God. This is to start "from below," where the first Christians started, by speaking of Jesus according to the human expressions he used to reveal his uniqueness to those who knew him in Palestine. Such a Christology of "ascent" will keep us from scandalizing the modern mind by presenting Jesus as simply the obedient executor of a preestablished plan, whose successful outcome he knew to be assured and which therefore involved no risk, no hesitation, no anguish. We will not, in other words, take away the capacity of Jesus to hope within the darkness of his own conflict with the authorities. Our contemporary Christ experience is precisely an invitation to take this historical struggle seriously. Too much traditional Christology began with Chalcedon and deduced from a highly static formula the interior attitudes of Jesus, thus rendering these attitudes static too, without development, change, or growth. Modern man will no longer accept this procedure, and it must consequently be rejected by any Christology which claims to speak to him.

In characterizing the Bible Abraham Heschel once said that it is far more important to have an anthropology for God than to have a theology for man. This remark has special relevance to our reading of the New Testament. For the self-transcendence obscurely sought for in man's present efforts to escape dehumanization is clearly a transcendence for *man,* and our problem is learning to speak about Jesus in such a way that his uniqueness is seen to reside in what God has accomplished in him as *man.* Jesus is God in so far as God identifies himself with Jesus for us; being man for God, Jesus is God for man. The moot point is, of course, whether such a finding of his divinity only in his humanity makes this divinity itself human and thereby rejects it. This question can be asked endlessly of anyone who adopts a Christology "from below," and this approach will consequently always have the burden of showing that Christ is not just a great leader or prophet but the definitive embodiment of God's true face toward mankind. Besides, it is always easier to argue about how one balances these two affirmations of Jesus than to devote one's energies to responding to his message. And this is no doubt why contemporary man is vastly more interested in the phenomenon of commitment in Jesus' life as well as his deep experience of the moral imperative. For no other characteristics so manifest the uniqueness of his love or the strength of his hope, virtues very much needed by those of us threatened by loss of nerve at the premature arrival of the future.

III

The significance of Jesus for the Christian, then, is that his relationship to the Father was achieved in and through his full acceptance of the human. His submission to all the limitations of life was precisely the means to his total openness to God. "Though he was in the form of God," says the great hymn of *Philippians*, "he did not deem equality with God something to be grasped at. Rather, he emptied himself and took the form of a slave, being born in the likeness of men. He was known to be of human estate, and it was thus that he humbled himself, obediently accepting even death, death on a cross! Because of this, God highly exalted him and bestowed on him the name above every other name, so that at Jesus' name every knee must bend in the heavens, on the earth, and under the earth, and every tongue proclaim to the glory of God the Father: Jesus Christ is Lord!"[15] Nothing is more mysterious than this need at times to be emptied by the experience of limitation before one can become aware of what is limitless and full. These are the times when life is indeed a burden, when human autonomy and control are at a loss, when to rely on anything less than God is to sense oneself less than man. Jesus knew of such times: "Come to me, all you who are weary and find life burdensome, and I will refresh you. Take my yoke upon your shoulders and learn from me."[16]

"Learn from me." In previous chapters I have made an effort to describe in some depth certain experiences whose significance can be radically altered by an effort to learn from Christ. The starting point has always been man himself, since whenever we confront ourselves as free and responsible agents we are confronting at one and the same time the activity of God in our lives; and by learning to love and believe in ourselves we learn to love and believe in God, in others, and in the world as well. Gilbert Chesterton once noted how ridiculous are people who speak of having been "through" things when it is evident that they have come out on the other side quite unchanged. "A man might have gone 'through' a plum pudding like a bullet. . . . The awful and sacred question is 'Has the pudding been through him?' "[17] Letting an experience go through us, however, is not as easy as it may sound. Most of us tend to live on the surface of our lives, content as long as the thin outer layer of our humanity yields up some meager harvest. We are all too willing to settle for the illusion of living instead of trying to discover our deepest truth. This is why the effort needed to turn our eyes inward upon the bewildering complexity of the human heart can bring both pain and confusion. But if we do make such an effort, then we need the support of knowing that Someone who loves us has seen it all before. This is what St. Paul meant when he said that God's Spirit "comes to the aid of our weakness. We do not even know how we ought to pray, but through our inarticulate groans the Spirit himself is pleading for us, and God, who searches our inmost being, knows what the Spirit means."[18]

I have tried to pursue this theme in one or other way throughout. Our new experience of the future terrifies us precisely because we have come to see it to be just as complex and unpredictable as the human heart itself. This future is now our own responsibility and we are not at all sure what we will do with it. As we saw in Chapter 1, Pierre Teilhard de Chardin was convinced that men and women today were in desperate need of some assurance to counteract a sense of hopelessness as well as the growing fear that technological progress is either going to stifle them in a straightjacket of control or bury them in the darkness of a mushroom cloud. Teilhard would have been the first to admit B. F. Skinner's recent claim that in modern life we are all manipulated. But he would insist that our problem is to find ways to preserve our freedom and dignity in spite of such inevitable manipulation. The key to this he saw to be love, and the key to love he saw to be Jesus. Just a year before Teilhard's death the Harvard sociologist Pitirim Sorokin wrote a lengthy study on this power of love. "Theoretically," he said, "love may have its own 'fission forces' that make its reservoir inexhaustible. When a person knows how to release these forces of love, he can spend love energy lavishly without exhausting his reservoir."[19] Sorokin was searching at the time for techniques of moral transformation, and he saw love's power as a purely natural phenomenon. But Teilhard saw it as *the* manifestation of the Christian phenomenon. For Christianity asserts that historically the love of one man has in fact been inexhaustible and continues to be, and that he alone can release its force to support that frailty of human love by which freedom becomes risk and progress insecurity. If people want some ultimate assurance that the human species can actually come together in more complex social structures without injuring the human person, then let them look to the example of Jesus and to his claim to be the life and absolute future of mankind.

I dealt at some length in the second chapter with today's yearning for social justice, because this peculiar human capacity to dream of better worlds is one of the clearest manifestations of the desire for self-transcendence. Yet it too has to be born in the experience of limitation. For the more freedom and imagination are restricted, the more do men and women seek to expose the myths upon which rest the power of injustice and hypocrisy. Jesus dreamt of the same transformation in Jewish society, and his conflict with the Temple authorities who opposed him led directly to his execution. Yet whether practically successful or not, such dreaming of the new is its own justification, as the teaching of Jesus amply testifies. This teaching can indeed be a prophetic witness, in so far as it issues in Christian proclamation and not in mere secular analysis or the absolutizing of legitimate but relative political options. Jesus' life shows too that no religious institution can escape the unfinished character of the human creature. Just as he criticized the religious leaders of his time, so his followers, while loving their church, must hold it accountable whenever it ignores new demands of the Gospel. This applies especially today to the rights of women and Blacks, and to the aspirations of people in the Third World. For history shows institutional religion to have been at times both socially blind and corrupt, with members and even some leaders who believed that, because they were not on the side of struggling man, they must be on the side of God. The gospel of Jesus, on the contrary, is a perennial rebuke to all those who lack the courage and boldness to dream the new, or who, because they love nobody, believe they love God.

The two more individual experiences I turned to in Chapters 3 and 4, those of play and failure, I have found remarkably visualized by the films of François Truffaut. These films now number thirteen and are all noted for their celebration of the joy of being human, in spite of their gentle insistence upon the pettiness and limitations of life. Truffaut is constantly reminding his audience how unfortunate someone is whose heart has not learned while young to hope, to love, and to put its trust in others. "People," exclaims one of his characters, "they're magnificent!" For Truffaut life is something to be received as a gift, not won as a prize, and his plots exemplify in startling ways what I have called in Chapter 3 the "game" of grace and in Chapter 4 the "logic" of Christian hope. No one can mistake the festivity of his stories, but for all their affirmation of the world's basic goodness, they are usually in danger of developing into conflict and misadventure, and sometimes actually do. In this they are very close to the Christian belief that surprise must be a central experience for anyone fully open to life, since God's action is wholly unpredictable and his purposes shrouded in mystery. Nowhere is this more evident than in the events of Jesus' own life story, in which, to our astonishment, the teaching which brought admiration from thousands led inexplicably to hatred and defeat. The thinnest possible membrane separated success from failure, with the *hosannas* and palms of a Sunday morning bringing cries for crucifixion on Friday afternoon. Yet this most unusual career of an itinerant preacher in Palestine has become, for the Christian, both normative and effective of God's graced presence to all humankind. And God's judgment on that career through the event of Easter morning shows to the eye of faith that in the game of life to lose is somehow also to win.

For large numbers of men and women today this sense of loss is most keenly felt through the coming of old age. Nothing so reminds us that "we are such stuff as dreams are made on, and our little life is rounded with a sleep." Before our present century very few ever had to learn to be human in this particular way. The poet Horace was one of these and addressed his friend Posthumus in poignant lines:

> Ah, Posthumus, my Posthumus, alas!
> The nimble-footed years, they pass, they pass . . .
>   Not all thy virtues will prevent
>   Old age, nor bid cold Death relent.

Old age was not an experience which Jesus himself had, so from this viewpoint his life can tell us nothing. But growing old is at root a "passion," a submission to the human condition in our time, and Jesus knew well what it meant to submit. "Father!" he cries out during his agony in the garden. "Everything is possible for you. Take this cup away from me. But let it be as you, not I, would have it."[20] Like each of us he could say with Isaiah, "You have folded up my life, like a weaver who severs the last thread."[21] The human courage of Jesus stands out in so startling a way precisely because the gospels make it clear at the start of his passion that he was afraid. "My heart is nearly broken with sorrow," he says in Matthew's account of Gethsemane. He "began to be filled with fear and distress," notes Mark. And Luke writes, "In his anguish he prayed with all the greater intensity, and his sweat became like drops of blood falling on the ground."[22] This is the same courage all of us need for facing life, as well as for growing old and for dying. Such courage demands values much higher than mere preservation of life. It demands that ultimate concern of Jesus for life's quality, his integrity in holding fast to an ideal, his capacity to forget himself in love for others, above all his unshakable confidence in the power of his Father to reverse that seemingly inescapable destiny of us all to end up in a dusty and eternal gloom.

A wise man once said that there comes a time in each of our lives when we do something or refrain from doing something, and that it is at this time we find out who we really are, that this is what we have been all our lives and what we will always be. I think this must also have been the experience of Jesus. The words of the psalmist would then have had significance for him as for no one else: "Truly you have formed my inmost being; you knit me in my mother's womb. I give you thanks that I am fearfully, wonderfully made."[23] Yet what God did in him as man he seeks to do in us as well. For Jesus is not the great anomaly among men and women but their greatest achievement, and this is why he brings to our sad and searching world a focus of hope that our efforts are indeed worthwhile to hold together the pieces of the earthly puzzle. He is our pledge that in the end we shall not be "caught" by life, that there will come a day when "he shall wipe every tear from their eyes, and there shall be no more death or mourning, crying out or pain."[24]

Teilhard de Chardin spoke of the world as a prison where people felt shut in and from which they desperately sought some way out. "The more the years pass," he admitted at the end of his life, "the more I recognize in myself and around me the great secret preoccupation of modern man: it is much less to dispute possession of the world than to find some means to escape from it."[25] This escape is made possible through Jesus, in whose humanity we see the flower of all our earthly endeavor, and in whose prophetic message we find the words of eternal life. Well may we take this message to be our one constant amid all the changes now taking place both in our dreams and in our fears. "Keep your attention closely fixed on it," says the second letter of Peter, "as you would on a lamp shining in a dark place until the first streaks of dawn appear and the morning star rises in your hearts."[26]

Notes

EXPLANATION

References to the Bible, unless otherwise indicated, are to the *New American Bible.* Abbreviations: Grail—*The Psalms: A New Translation;* JB —*The Jerusalem Bible;* NEB—*The New English Bible;* Knox—The Ronald Knox translation; RSV—*Revised Standard Version.*

INTRODUCTION

1 New York: Vanguard Press, 1973.
2 See Robert J. Lifton, *Boundaries: Psychological Man in Revolution* (New York: Vintage, 1970), 37–63; Richard R. Niebuhr, *Experiential Religion* (New York: Harper & Row, 1972), *passim.*
3 Philip Rieff, *The Triumph of the Therapeutic* (New York: Harper & Row, 1966), 243, 261. See, as a comparison, the perceptive study by John B. Orr and F. Patrick Nichelson, *The Radical Suburb* (Philadelphia: Westminster Press, 1970).
4 C. G. Jung, *Modern Man in Search of a Soul* (New York: Harcourt, Brace & World, Harvest edition, 1966), 42.
5 Karl Rahner, "Theology and Anthropology," *The Word in History,* ed. T. Patrick Burke (New York: Sheed & Ward, 1966), 1–23. See also on this approach Piet Fransen, "Grace, Theologizing and the Humanizing of Man," *Proceedings of the Catholic Theological Society of America* XXVII (1972), 55–77; Piet Schoonenberg, *The Christ* (New York: Herder & Herder, 1971), 13–49.
6 *Confessions* III, 6, 11.

7   Pierre Teilhard de Chardin, *Christianity and Evolution* (New York: Harcourt Brace Jovanovich, 1969), 28.

8   This point has been developed at greater length by William F. Lynch, *Christ and Prometheus* (Notre Dame, Ind.: Notre Dame University Press, 1970), 7 ff.

9   Blaise Pascal, *Pensées,* trans. Martin Turnell (New York: Harper & Row, 1962), no. 116.

10 Langdon Gilkey, *Naming the Whirlwind* (New York: Bobbs-Merrill, 1969), 352–53.

11 John 16:23.

CHAPTER I

1   C. E. Black, *The Dynamics of Modernization* (New York: Harper Torchbook edition, 1967), 1, 4.

2   Pierre Teilhard de Chardin, *Science and Christ* (New York: Harper & Row, 1968), 128–29.

3   *Letters from a Traveller* (New York: Harper & Row, 1962), 202.

4   Erik H. Erikson, "Memorandum on Youth" in *Toward the Year 2000, vol. 96 of Daedalus* (1967), 864.

5   For example, Erich Fromm, *The Revolution of Hope* (New York: Harper & Row, 1968).

6   Jacques Monod, *Chance and Necessity* (New York: Knopf, 1971), 172–73.

7   See the interview published in the *New York Times,* March 15, 1971.

8   Gibson Winter, *Being Free* (New York: Macmillan, 1970), 22.

9   Ibid., 94.

10 Pierre Teilhard de Chardin, *The Phenomenon of Man* (New York: Harper & Row, 1965), 228–29. Hereafter cited as *PM.*

11 Ibid., 231.

12 Ibid., 233.

13 "Le Christique," an unpublished essay.

14 *PM,* 171.

15 Ibid., 223.

16 Pierre Teilhard de Chardin, *The Future of Man* (New York: Harper & Row, 1964), 294.

17 Ibid., 275–76.

18 Pierre Teilhard de Chardin, *The Activation of Energy* (New York: Harcourt Brace Jovanovitch, 1971), 73–74.

19 *The Vision of the Past* (New York: Harper & Row, 1967), 137. I am indebted here to the unpublished doctoral dissertation of Francis X. Winters, "Teilhard de Chardin's Morality of Movement," defended at Fordham University.

20 *PM,* 262. For a more thorough development of this idea see Christopher F. Mooney, *Teilhard de Chardin and the Mystery of Christ* (New York: Harper & Row, 1966), 46–55.

21 *PM,* 262.

22 Ibid., 264–65.

23 Ibid., 233.

24 Ibid., 270.

25 *Future of Man,* 180–81.

26 Pierre Teilhard de Chardin, *The Divine Milieu* (New York: Harper & Row, 1960), 54, 61.

27 This last statement is the conclusion of a very lengthy theological analysis of the incarnation within an evolutionary system of thought. Teilhard's position is given in Mooney, op. cit., 67–86.

28 *PM,* 296.

29 Pierre Teilhard de Chardin, *Human Energy* (New York: Harcourt Brace Jovanovitch, 1971), 157–58.

30 *Réflexions sur le bonheur* (Paris: Seuil, 1960), 67–70.

31 *Future of Man,* 19, 21.

32 *PM,* 288–89.

33 Pierre Teilhard de Chardin, *Hymn of the Universe* (New York: Harper & Row, 1965), 29.

34 Ibid.

CHAPTER 2

1 Jonas Salk, *The Survival of the Wisest* (New York: Harper & Row, 1973). See the discussion between Salk and others in *Center Report* VI (1973), 3–8.

2 Amos N. Wilder, "The Rhetoric of Ancient and Modern Apocalyptic," *Interpretation* XXV (1971), 444.

3 William A. Beardslee, *A House for Hope* (Philadelphia: Westminster Press, 1972), 12, 109.

4 John O'Manique, "On the Possibility of a New Man," *Teilhard Review* VIII (1973), 50–51.

5 B. F. Skinner, *Beyond Freedom and Dignity* (New York: Knopf, 1971).

6 Karl Rahner, "Christianity and the New Man," in his *Theological Investigations,* (Baltimore: Helicon Press, 1966), V: 138.

7 See Ray L. Hart, *Unfinished Man and the Imagination* (New York: Herder & Herder, 1968).

8 *Pastoral Constitution on the Church in the Modern World,* arts. 54, 55, in Walter M. Abbot and Joseph Gallagher, eds., *The Documents of Vatican II* (New York: Guild Press, 1966).

9 See Rahner, op. cit., 144–45.

10 John Macquarrie, *The Concept of Peace* (New York: Harper & Row, 1973), 27.

11 Quoted by Roger L. Shinn in his *Wars and Rumors of Wars* (Nashville, Tenn.: Abingdon Press, 1972), 235.

12 Norman O. Brown, *Life Against Death* (Middletown, Conn.: Wesleyan University Press, 1970), 101. See pp. 87–109 for the interpretation of Freud given here.

13   Hannah Arendt, *On Revolution* (New York: Viking Compass edition, 1971), 8.

14   See for this approach James V. Schall, "Religion and Development —a Minority View," *Worldview* (July 1973), 35–40.

15   The summary sketch here is that of Robert McAfee Brown, "The Frontier of Revolution," in his *Frontiers for the Church Today* (New York: Oxford University Press, 1973), 48–64. For a more extended treatment of this perspective see Gustavo Gutierrez, *A Theology of Liberation* (Maryknoll, N.Y.: Orbis, 1971), 21–42; 81–99.

16   Paulo Freire, *The Pedagogy of the Oppressed* (New York: Herder & Herder, 1970), 19.

17   Hannah Arendt, *On Violence* (New York: Harcourt, Brace & World, 1970), 56, 79.

18   This expressive meaning of violence, in contrast to its instrumental meaning, is advocated by Franz Fanon, *The Wretched of the Earth* (New York: Grove Press, 1968). See also the treatment in Shinn, op. cit., 235–78.

19   Karl Rahner, "The Theology of Power," *Theological Investigations,* (Baltimore: Helicon Press, 1966), IV: 401.

20   Rahner, op. cit., 150.

21   Thomas E. Clarke, "Holiness and Justice in Tension," *The Way* XIII (1973), 188.

22   Gutierrez, op. cit., 13.

23   Quoted ibid., 10.

24   For further elaboration of this approach see Edward Schillebeeckx, *God the Future of Man* (New York: Sheed & Ward, 1968), 185 ff.

25   S. G. F. Brandon makes this claim in *Jesus and the Zealots* (New York: Scribners, 1967), but the contrary evidence is overwhelming, as George R. Edwards has shown in his *Jesus and the Politics of Violence* (New York: Harper & Row, 1971). See also Oscar Cullmann, *Jesus and the Revolutionaries* (New York: Harper & Row, 1970).

26   John T. Pawlikowski has explored in depth this relationship between Jesus and the Pharisees in "On Renewing the Revolution of the Pharisees: A New Approach to Theology and Politics," *Cross Currents* XX (1970), 415–34. See also his more popular presentation: "Jesus and the Revolutionaries," *Christian Century,* December 6, 1972.

27   Matthew 21:33–46; Mark 12:1–12; Luke 20:9–19. C. H. Dodd, among others, gives such an interpretation of Jesus' last days in *The Founder of Christianity* (New York: Macmillan, 1970), 137–62.

28   A fuller development of this outlook will be found in Gutierrez, op. cit., 229–38.

29   See Elise Boulding's treatment of the thought of the Dutch scholar Fred Polak, who deals at length with this impairment of the contemporary imagination, in her "Futurology and the Imaging Capacity

of the West," *Teilhard Review* VII (1972), 12–23.

30 Romans 8:24–25 (Knox).

CHAPTER 3

1   Franz Alexander, "A Contribution to the Theory of Play," *Psycho-analytic Quarterly* XXVII (1958), 192. Quoted by Robert E. Neale, *In Praise of Play* (New York: Harper & Row, 1969), 164. See also pp. 12–16.

2   Plato, *Laws*, VII, 803. Quoted by Hugo Rahner, *Man at Play* (New York: Herder & Herder, 1967), 13.

3   Friedrich Schiller, *On the Aesthetic Education of Man* (Oxford: Clarendon Press, 1967), 107.

4   Johan Huizinga, *Homo Ludens, A Study of the Play Element in Culture* (Boston: Beacon Press, 1955), ix, 46.

5   Josef Pieper, *In Tune with the World* (New York: Harcourt, Brace & World, 1965), 3.

6   Romano Guardini, *The Spirit of the Liturgy* (New York: Benziger, 1931), 99.

7   Erik H. Erikson, *Childhood and Society* (New York: W. W. Norton, 1963), 214.

8   The playing child, on the contrary, does not move aside from reality but "advances forward to new stages of mastery. I propose the theory that the child's play is the infantile form of the human ability to deal with experience by creating model situations and to master reality by experiment and planning." Ibid., 222.

9   Huizinga, op. cit., 191, 75.

10 Neale, op. cit., 43. I summarize here his masterly chapter on play as adventure, pp. 42–69.

11 Huizinga, op. cit., 2–4.

12 Friedrich Nietzsche, *Gesammelte Werke* (Munich, 1922), IX: 480. Quoted by Pieper, op. cit., 10.

13 Ted L. Estess, quoted by David L. Miller, *Gods and Games* (New York: Harper & Row, 1973), xxv.

14 Nietzsche, op. cit., XVI: 37; XIX: 352. Quoted by Pieper, op. cit., 20.

15 Dag Hammarskjöld, *Markings* (New York: Knopf, 1966), 89, 205.

16 Harvey Cox, *The Feast of Fools* (Cambridge, Mass.: Harvard University Press, 1969), 26.

17 Hugo Rahner, op. cit., 9, 4. I have transcribed the Greek characters here into English.

18 Aristotle, *Nicomachean Ethics,* IV, 14, 1128a. Quoted by Rahner, op. cit., 94.

19 See Rahner, op. cit., 2, 99–104.

20 See for example, Jürgen Moltmann, "How Can I Play in a Strange

Land?" in his *Theology of Play* (New York: Harper & Row, 1972); Pieter Geyl, "Huizinga as Accuser of His Age," in his *Encounters in History* (London: Collins, 1963).

21 Huizinga, op. cit., 192.
22 Moltmann, op. cit., 2.
23 Quoted by Rahner, op. cit., 97–98.
24 Proverbs 8:30–31. New American Bible translation.
25 Quoted by Rahner, op. cit., 25.
26 Boris Pasternak, *Doctor Zhivago* (New York: Pantheon, 1958), 12–13.
27 II Corinthians 1:19–20.
28 Guardini, op. cit., 102.
29 Josef Pieper, *Leisure: The Basis of Culture* (New York: Mentor-Omega, 1963), 41.
30 Douglas V. Steere, "Contemplation and Leisure," *Humanitas* VIII (1972), 289.
31 *Summa Theologica,* pars I–II, ques. 32, art. 7. See on this question the discussion in Pieper, *Leisure,* 97–105.
32 Pieper, *In Tune,* 30–31.
33 Matthew 18:3.
34 Rahner, op. cit., 65.

CHAPTER 4

1   Daniel Boorstin, *The Image; or, What Happened to the American Dream* (New York: Atheneum, 1962), 3–4.
2   As reported in the *New York Times* for December 1, 1973, 35.
3   Erik H. Erikson, *Childhood and Society* (New York: W. W. Norton, 1963), 292, 286. His whole eighth chapter deals with "Reflections on the American Identity." The interpretation followed here is that of Don S. Browning in *Generative Man: Psychoanalytic Perspectives* (Philadelphia: Westminster Press, 1973), 173–77.
4   William F. Lynch, *Christ and Prometheus* (Notre Dame, Ind.: Notre Dame University Press, 1970), 20.
5   See Rona and Laurence Cherry, "Depression," *New York Times Magazine,* November 25, 1973.
6   C. G. Jung, *Modern Man in Search of a Soul* (New York: Harcourt, Brace & World, Harvest Book edition, 1966), 102.
7   Ibid., 66.
8   S. I. Hayakawa, *Symbol, Status and Personality* (Harcourt Brace Jovanovich, 1963), 81. Quoted by Elizabeth O'Connor in *Our Many Selves* (New York: Harper & Row, 1971), 143.
9   Sirach 10:27–28.
10 Paul Ricoeur, *Fallible Man* (Chicago: Regnery, 1965), 93–103.
11 Ibid., 199–200. See also 188–91.
12 Marc Oraison, *Illusion and Anxiety* (New York: Macmillan, 1963), 78.

13   Erich Fromm, *Man for Himself* (New York: Rinehart, 1947), 40.
     Quoted in Browning, op. cit., 115.

14   Erik H. Erikson, *Young Man Luther* (New York: W. W. Norton,
     1958), 208–9. Quoted in Browning, op. cit., 198.

15   Ibid., 157.

16   Erik H. Erikson, *Identity and the Life Cycle* (New York: International
     Universities Press, 1959), 55–74. The interpretation is that of
     Browning, op. cit., 182–83.

17   Romans 5:17, 20–21 (RSV).

18   Paul Ricoeur, "Guilt, Ethics and Religion," in *Moral Evil Under
     Challenge,* Concilium: Theology in the Age of Renewal, vol. LVI,
     ed. Johannes B. Metz (New York: Herder & Herder, 1970), 24.
     See also Ricoeur's treatment of this question in "Hope and the
     Structure of Philosophical Systems," *Proceedings of the American Cath-
     olic Philosophical Association* XLIV (1970), 55–69.

19   Isaiah 43:19.

20   Romans 11:32–33.

21   *Summa Theologica* II–II, 163, 2; *De Malo,* 16, 3.

22   Blaise Pascal, *Pensées,* trans. Martin Turnell (New York: Harper &
     Row, 1962), no. 383. Arnold Uleyn cites the passage in this context
     in his excellent chapter on the importance of confession in *Is It I,
     Lord?* (New York: Holt, Rinehart & Winston, 1969), 22–44.

23   Romans 7:15.

24   On the classic biblical texts of chaps. 2 and 3 of Genesis and chap.
     5 of Romans, see Henricus Renkens, *Israel's Concept of the Beginning*
     (New York: Herder & Herder, 1964), and Piet Schoonenberg,
     Man and Sin (Notre Dame, Ind.: Fides, 1965).

25   I John 1:8–9.

26   II Corinthians 5:21.

27   Paul Ricoeur, quoted by Uleyn, op. cit., 75. See also Ricoeur,
     "Guilt, Ethics and Religion," 15–25.

28   I find it quite astounding that in *Whatever Became of Sin?* (New York:
     Hawthorn, 1973) so perceptive a Christian as Karl Menninger
     could write a whole book on this concept and hardly mention the
     central Christian assertion that what God ultimately wants to do
     with sin is to forgive it. This is not to deny the validity of Mennin-
     ger's keen analysis of the loss of a sense of sin today, especially sins
     of political corruption, the inhumanity of our penal system, the
     callousness of war, the manipulation of the underprivileged, etc.
     And his placing of sexual sins in their proper perspective is admira-
     ble. But his tone is that of the stern moralist; the big sinners to
     whom he points his indignant finger are not likely to be listening,
     while readers who are conscious of their frailty will learn little about
     the treatment they can expect from God.

29   Jeremiah 17:9; Isaiah 41:13–14.

30 Herbert Butterfield, *Christianity and History* (New York: Scribner's, 1949), 76.
31 Psalm 103:13–14 (Grail).

CHAPTER 5

1 Leonard Davis, "Today's Retirees," *Modern Maturity* (June-July 1973), 19.
2 Simone de Beauvoir, *The Coming of Age* (New York: Putnam, 1972), 5.
3 *Poems and Prose of Gerard Manley Hopkins,* 4th Edition, edited by W. M. Gardner & M. H. MacKenzie (New York & Oxford University Press, 1967), 88–89.
4 Erik H. Erikson, *Insight and Responsibility* (New York: W. W. Norton, 1964), 132.
5 de Beauvoir, op. cit., 505.
6 Erik H. Erikson, *Identity and the Life Cycle* (New York: International Universities Press, 1959), 98.
7 Ibid.
8 Ibid., 56. Observations similar to these are made also in his *Childhood and Society* (New York: W. W. Norton, 1963), 268–69.
9 Erikson, *Insight and Responsibility,* 133–34.
10 Ibid.
11 William Meissner, "Notes on the Psychology of Faith," *Journal of Religion and Health* VIII (1969), 57–58.
12 Erik H. Erikson, *Young Man Luther* (New York: W. W. Norton, 1958), 112.
13 Meissner, op. cit., 59.
14 Victor Frankl, *Man's Search for Meaning* (New York: Pocket Books edition, 1963), 122.
15 Ibid., 190–91. See also his *The Doctor and the Soul* (New York: Knopf, 1957) for further elaboration.
16 Karl Rahner, "The Comfort of Time," in his *Theological Investigations,* (Baltimore: Helicon Press, 1967), III: 145.
17 Ibid., 155.
18 Frankl, *Man's Search for Meaning,* 175: Alfons Deeken has emphasized this need of self-transcendence in old age in his pages on how to grow old gracefully: *Growing Old, and How to Cope with It* (New York: Paulist Press, 1972), 21–103.
19 See the beautiful essay by Romano Guardini, "Faith as Overcoming," in his *The Faith and Modern Man* (New York: Pantheon, 1952), 83–92.
20 II Corinthians 4:7–9.
21 Pierre Teilhard de Chardin, *Writings in Time of War* (New York: Harper & Row, 1968), 242.
22 *Activation of Energy* (New York: Harcourt Brace Jovanovich, 1971), 248–49.

23   *The Divine Milieu* (New York, Harper & Row, 1960), 88.

24   Pierre Teilhard de Chardin and Maurice Blondel, *Correspondence* (New York: Herder & Herder, 1967), 35.

25   Pierre Teilhard de Chardin, *The Making of a Mind* (New York: Harper & Row, 1965), 275.

26   Teilhard, *Divine Milieu,* 82. Teilhard's most extensive treatment of the "passivities of diminishment" appears here on pages 80–93.

27   Ibid., 90–93.

28   Psalm 71:5–9, 20–22 (Grail).

29   II Corinthians 12:10, 9.

30   See, for example, the publication of hearings before the Senate's Special Committee on Aging on June 19 and 21, 1973; or articles like "Waiting for the End: On Nursing Homes," *New York Times Magazine,* March 31, 1974, and "Poverty and Pride Trap City's Aged," *New York Times,* September 7, 1973.

31   See Margaret H. and S. Allen Bacon, "Time to Retire?" *Christian Century,* February 14, 1973, 201–4.

32   C. G. Jung, *Modern Man in Search of His Soul* (New York: Harcourt, Brace World, 1966), 109–110.

33   Guardini, op. cit., 89.

CHAPTER 6

1   See the development of this theme by Walter Kasper, "Christian Humanism," in *Religion and the Humanizing of Man,* ed. James M. Robinson (Los Angeles: Council on the Study of Religion, 1972), 20 ff. On the phenomena of obsession and concealment see the essays in *Death and Identity,* ed. Robert Fulton (New York: Wiley, 1965).

2   For example, the English sociologist Geoffrey Gorer, in his *Death, Grief and Mourning* (New York: Doubleday Anchor Book edition, 1967), 192–99; and the American theologian William F. May, "The Sacral Power of Death in Contemporary Experience," in *Perspectives on Death,* ed. Liston O. Mills (Nashville, Tenn.: Abingdon Press, 1969), 168–196.

3   May, op. cit., 172.

4   Jessica Mitford, *The American Way of Death* (New York: Simon & Schuster, 1963), 14.

5   See the incisive discussion by William F. Lynch, "Death as Nothingness," *Continuum* V (1967), 459–69.

6   Paul Tillich, *The Courage To Be* (New Haven: Yale University Press, 1952), 41.

7   James M. Demske, "Heidegger: Wisdom as Death," *Continuum* V (1967), 509.

8   Karl Rahner, "On Christian Dying," in his *Theological Investigations* (New York: Herder & Herder, 1971), VII: 287–88. See also James T. Laney, "Ethics and Death," in *Perspectives on Death,* 231–52. It

should be noted that outlooks such as that of Gerald Feinberg in *The Prometheus Project* (New York: Doubleday, 1968) miss this whole point by assuming that man would really want a life which could be prolonged indefinitely by the future resources of science; whereas it is precisely *time* that prevents man from becoming his definitive self, and what he really wants is liberation from it.

9   Jacques Choron deals well with these meanings *in* life in *Death and Modern Man* (New York: Collier, 1972), 169–77.

10   Elizabeth Kübler-Ross, *On Death and Dying* (New York: Macmillan, 1970).

11   Carl G. Jung, "The Soul and Death," in *The Meaning of Death,* ed. Herman Feifel (New York: McGraw-Hill, 1965), 6.

12   Kübler-Ross, op. cit., 265–66.

13   This point is well made by H. A. Williams, *True Resurrection* (New York: Holt, Rinehart & Winston, 1972), 172–73.

14   Lynch, op. cit., 467.

15   On the approach taken here see Michael Schmaus, "Death as Fulfillment," *Continuum* V (1967), 483–88; Karl Rahner, op. cit., 289–90.

16   Luke 23:46.

17   Romans 6:3 ff.

18   See Karl Rahner's treatment of the sacraments as encounters with the death of Christ in *On the Theology of Death* (New York: Herder & Herder, 1962), 80–88.

19   II Corinthians 4:10. See Philippians 3:10–11.

20   II Timothy 2:11.

21   Peter Berger, *A Rumor of Angels* (New York: Doubleday, 1969).

22   William James, *The Varieties of Religious Experience* (New York: Collier Books edition, 1967), 356.

23   I Corinthians 2:9; Romans 8:24. See Williams, op. cit., 177–78, and Wolfhart Pannenberg, *What Is Man?* (Philadelphia: Fortress Press, 1970), 49–53.

24   See the extended treatment by Oscar Cullmann, *Immortality of the Soul or Resurrection of the Dead?* (London: Epworth Press, 1958), and the theological history of the two images in Milton McC. Gatch, *Death: Meaning and Mortality in Christian Thought and Contemporary Culture* (New York: Seabury Press, 1969).

25   Pierre Benoît, "Resurrection: At the End of Time or Immediately After Death?" *Concilium* LX, *Immortality and Resurrection* (New York: Herder & Herder, 1970), 110–14. The difficulty of course, as Benoît's title indicates, is that, while Paul knows nothing of an immortal soul, he never reconciled the final resurrection of the dead on the Day of Yahweh with the risen Christ's present victory over death and the implications of this for the individual Christian.

26   These ideas are developed in many essays. For example, *The Future*

of Man (New York: Harper & Row, 1964), 47–52, 87–89, 103–123; *Science and Christ* (New York: Harper & Row, 1968), 92–97, 192–196; *Activation of Energy* (New York: Harcourt Brace Jovanovich, 1971), 329–337; *Man's Place in Nature* (New York: Harper & Row, 1966), 17–36.

27 *Future of Man,* 121. Slight corrections have been made here based on the original in *L'Avenir de l'homme* (Paris: Seuil, 1959), 154.

28 Albert Camus, *The Myth of Sisyphus* (New York: Vintage edition, 1955); Norbert Wiener, *The Human Use of Human Beings* (London: Eyre & Spottiswoode, 1954); Jacques Monod, *Chance and Necessity* (New York: Knopf, 1971). See the discussion of Monod in the first part of chap. 1 of this volume.

29 *Activation of Energy,* 403. See also ibid., 183–95, 397–406.

30 On death as a paroxysm of consciousness outside space and time, see *Activation of Energy* 46, 335, 392; *Future of Man,* 123, 302. On Teilhard's eloquent attack upon apathy and boredom, see *Future of Man,* 146, 206.

31 *Activation of Energy,* 190.

32 Ibid., 404.

33 See Christopher F. Mooney, *Teilhard de Chardin and the Mystery of Christ* (New York: Harper & Row, 1966), 113–21.

34 *Divine Milieu* (New York: Harper & Row, 1960), 61.

35 *Future of Man,* 148.

CHAPTER 7

1 II Corinthians 5:19 (RSV).

2 Edward Schillebeeckx, "Theology of Renewal Talks about God," *Theology of Renewal Proceedings,* ed. L. K. Shook (New York: Herder & Herder, 1968), I:95–96.

3 Kenneth Keniston, *The Uncommitted* (New York: Harcourt, Brace & World, 1965), 422.

4 Contrast this anxiety among scientists today with the serene optimism attributed to them over a decade ago by C. P. Snow in *The Two Cultures and the Scientific Revolution* (Cambridge, Eng.: The University Press, 1959).

5 Leander E. Keck and James E. Sellers, "Theological Ethics in an American Crisis," *Interpretation* XXIV (1970), 479.

6 Harvey Cox, *The Feast of Fools* (Cambridge, Mass.: Harvard University Press, 1969), 142.

7 I Corinthians 1:25.

8 See on this question Philip Hefner, "The Relocation of the God-Question," *Lutheran Quarterly* XXI (1969), 327–41; John B. Cobb, Jr., "The Population Explosion and the Rights of the Subhuman World," *IDOC International,* September 12, 1970, 40–62.

9   James H. Cone, "Black Consciousness and Black Church," *Christianity and Crisis* XXX (1970), 246.

10 Gibson Winter, *Being Free* (New York: Macmillan, 1970), 125.

11 Frederick Herzog, "Theology of Liberation," *Continuum* VII (1970), 519.

12 W. Norman Pittenger, *Christology Reconsidered* (London: S.C.M. Press, 1970), 65.

13 Karl Rahner has exposed at some length the mythological character of much contemporary understanding of Chalcedon in his "Current Problems in Christology," in his *Theological Investigations* (Baltimore: Helicon Press, 1961), I:149–200.

14 Edward Schillebeeckx, "Persoonlijke openbaringsgestalte van de Vader," *Tijdschrift voor Theologie* VI (1966), 277. This very rich article has been quoted at length in Robert North, "Soul-Body Unity and God-Man Unity," *Theological Studies* XXX (1969), 27–60. A far more systematic exposition, from the Roman Catholic side, of the contemporary pastoral difficulties with Chalcedon is given by Piet Schoonenberg, *The Christ* (New York: Herder & Herder, 1971). See also John A. T. Robinson's survey of the longer-standing Protestant appreciation of these difficulties in *The Human Face of God* (Philadelphia: Westminster Press, 1973).

15 Philippians 2:6–11.

16 Matthew 11:28–29.

17 Gilbert K. Chesterton, "The Contented Man," in *A Miscellany of Men* (New York: Dodd, Mead, 1912), 303.

18 Romans 8:26–27 (NEB).

19 Pitirim A. Sorokin, *The Ways and Power of Love* (Boston: Beacon Press 1954), 26.

20 Mark 14:36 (JB).

21 Isaiah 38:12.

22 Matthew 26:38; Mark 14:34; Luke 22:44.

23 Psalm 139:13–14.

24 Revelation 21:4.

25 Pierre Teilhard de Chardin, "Le Coeur de la matière," an unpublished essay.

26 II Peter 1:19.

MAY 2 9 84